MERSEY PORTS
LIVERPOOL & BIRKENHEAD

MERSEY PORTS
LIVERPOOL & BIRKENHEAD

Ian Collard

TEMPUS

First published 2001
Reprinted 2002, 2006

Tempus Publishing Limited
The Mill, Brimscombe Port,
Stroud, Gloucestershire, GL5 2QG

© Ian Collard, 2001

British Library Cataloguing in Publication Data.
A catalogue record for this book is available from the British Library.

ISBN 0 7524 2110 7

Typesetting and origination by Tempus Publishing Limited
Printed and bound in Great Britain

Contents

Acknowledgements

I would like to thank the various shipping lines that have given me valuable help and assistance in preparing and researching this piece of work. Also, the support I have been given by friends and family has helped me to concentrate on the objective of compiling a record of industrial activity in one of the great ports of the world.

Introduction

This book celebrates the River Mersey, the Port Authority and the ships that have visited the river; it is a record of maritime life on a great river over a time of change and upheaval. The River Mersey, its buildings, architecture and docks have provided a backdrop to many of the significant events that have occurred on Merseyside over the years

I first became interested in ships when I was taken on a Liverpool Corporation Transport tour of the dock system in the 1950s. Every conceivable type of vessel, representative of shipping companies worldwide, occupied nearly every berth on the docks.

I distinctly recall the Cunard White Star motor ship, *Britannic*, loading cargo for New York at Huskisson Branch No.1 Dock in the final years of her eventful life. I also remember standing on the promenade at New Brighton watching her move gracefully down the river on her last passenger sailing. Life those days was dominated by 'first' and 'last' sailings by liners, cargo and coastal vessels.

The *Britannic* left the sister ships *Sylvania* and *Carinthia* to continue the New York and Canadian services supplemented by the smaller *Parthia* and *Media*. Canadian Pacific operated the *Empress of Britain*, *Empress of England* and the *Empress of France*, which was replaced by the *Empress of Canada* in 1961.

Anchor Line owned the *Caledonia*, *Circassia* and *Cilicia* which operated on passenger services to India. The Bibby Line vessels also loaded at Birkenhead Docks and carried passengers and cargo to Port Said, Port Sudan, Aden, Colombo and Rangoon.

The port provided facilities to a host of international shipping companies but was home to the ships of the Blue Funnel, Ellerman, Harrison, Elder Dempster Lines and many other vessels.

Princes Landing Stage provided a focal point to the activity at the port. It was not unusual in those days to see two passenger liners berthed at the stage with another anchored in the river waiting to berth later in the day.

New motor vessels replaced the old Mersey ferries in the fifties and the sixties and the leisure and business traveller soon adopted these. Some, like the famous *Royal Iris*, came to represent Merseyside and served her owners well until her retirement in 1994.

The Mersey also became the accepted second home for the ships of the Isle of Man Steam Packet Company. They used Liverpool as their principal mainland port and the bulk of their fleet was wintered in Morpeth Dock at Birkenhead from September to May the following year.

I vividly remember standing on the Princes Landing Stage on a blustery May morning in 1962 to witness the new *Manx Maid* sail on her maiden voyage to Douglas, Isle of Man. Several years later I had the pleasure of sailing on the maiden voyage of her sister ship *Ben my Chree*. Both are now just memories as are the centenary vessel *Lady of Mann*, *Manxman*, *Mona's Isle* and other vessels of that class.

Modern roll-on/roll-off car ferries, which linked Liverpool with Dublin and Belfast, replaced the classic coastal passenger vessels *Leinster*, *Munster*, *Ulster Prince* and *Ulster Monarch*. These ships are now a fond memory – as are the *Irish Coast*, *Scottish Coast* and *St Clair*. I had the pleasure of sailing on the latter on a positioning voyage from Aberdeen to Liverpool in the sixties when she provided a winter relief service on the Liverpool to Belfast service as the two regular vessels were overhauled.

However, as old friends came to the end of their useful life or became uneconomical to operate they were replaced by new vessels which soon became part of the life of the river. We now have the Seacats sailing to Douglas, *Mersey Viking* and *Lagan Viking* to Belfast and P&O vessels sailing twice a day in and out of the Port.

The Royal Seaforth Dock can turn around the largest container vessel in just twelve hours and provides the most up-to-date facilities imagined for shipowners who use the Port.

Ship repair work is alive and well on Merseyside. Northwestern Shiprepairers provides facilities for refits and overhauls for vessels of the Stena Line, Irish Ferries, Norse Merchant and P&O at their yards in Birkenhead and drydock in Liverpool.

In recent years the river and its docks have provided the setting for the Tall Ships, Battle of the Atlantic and the visits of the *Queen Elizabeth 2*. Consequently the port is a living entity and therefore continues to prosper and thrive. A walk along the banks of the river at high water provides evidence of how the port has been able to adapt to the shipping revolution of the sixties and the seventies. Although many of the docks that were operative at that time are now empty and closed the main activity of the port has moved towards the sea at Seaforth.

In 2004 thirty-two million tonnes of cargo was handled, the port has improved rail and road links including a Channel Tunnel Freight Terminal. It provides shipping services to the Iberian Peninsular, the Continent, Mediterranean, Ireland, Scandinavia and the Baltic and is still the principal United Kingdom port for the North Atlantic and Canadian trade.

The Port of Liverpool has a rich maritime history but has also shown in recent years a determination to be flexible and responsive to changing needs. The Mersey Docks & Harbour Company is clearly striving to ensure that customers have the facilities they require by developing new systems which improve performance in handling containers, grain, timber and other cargos.

I look forward with confidence to witnessing the port taking advantage of the opportunities that new developments and technology have to offer over the next thirty years. The Port of Liverpool will survive and prosper and the ships and docks will continue to provide employment and enjoyment to the people of the region and to those who visit by road, rail and sea.

It has provided me with an interest that has dominated my life at times and has given me many happy memories of events, some of which I have been able to capture on film. I hope the photographs in this book help to remind people of the variety of ships that have sailed up the river and the influence this maritime tradition has had on the customs and culture of life in one of the great maritime ports of the world.

The Port of Liverpool

Legend:

1. Gladstone Dock
2. Hornby Dock
3. Alexandra Dock
4. Langton Dock
5. Brocklebank Dock
6. Canada Dock
7. Graving Dock
8. Huskisson Dock
9. Sandon H/T Dock
10. Wellington Dock
11. Bramley-Moore Dock
12. Nelson Dock
13. Collingwood Dock
14. Salisbury Dock
15. Trafalgar Dock
16. East Waterloo Dock
17. West Waterloo Dock
18. Prince H/T Dock
19. Princes Dock
20. Alfred Dock
21. Vittoria Dock
22. East Float
23. West Float
24. Graving Dock
25. Bidston Dock
● Freeport Park Units
● Maritime Centre
● Rail Terminal
● Timber Terminal
● Grain Terminal
● Liverpool Landing Stage
● Pier Head
● Tower Quays
● Tranmere Oil Stages

Area for Future Development

Container Terminal

Royal Seaforth Dock

To M57, M58
M62, M6
A5036

A565

A567

Branch Dock No.1
Branch Dock No.2
Branch Dock No.3

REDCO LTD

Port of Liverpool Building

River Mersey

Liverpool Dock Estate

☐ Liverpool Freeport
☐ Dock Estate

Birkenhead Dock Estate

A554
A41

M53

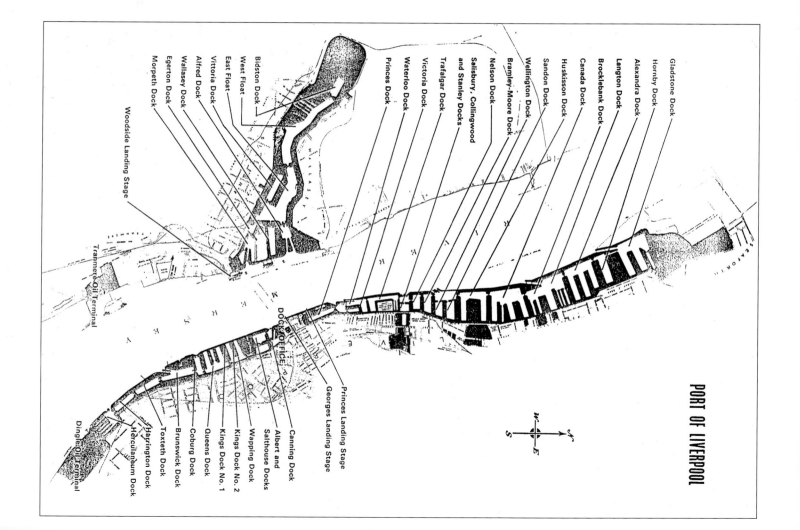

PORT OF LIVERPOOL

Gladstone Dock
Hornby Dock
Alexandra Dock
Langton Dock
Brocklebank Dock
Canada Dock
Huskisson Dock
Sandon Dock
Wellington Dock
Bramley-Moore Dock
Nelson Dock
Salisbury, Collingwood and Stanley Docks
Trafalgar Dock
Victoria Dock
Waterloo Dock
Princes Dock

Bidston Dock
West Float
East Float
Vittoria Dock
Alfred Dock
Wallasey Dock
Egerton Dock
Morpeth Dock

Woodside Landing Stage

Tranmere Oil Terminal

DOCK OFFICE

Princes Landing Stage
Georges Landing Stage
Canning Dock
Albert and Salthouse Docks
Waping Dock
Kings Dock No. 2
Kings Dock No. 1
Queens Dock
Coburg Dock
Brunswick Dock
Toxteth Dock
Harrington Dock
Herculaneum Dock

Dingle Oil Terminal

One

The Docks

The earliest record of the River Mersey is to be found in a deed dated 1002, in the reign of Ethelred. The deeds, which later passed into the possession of Edward the Confessor, bequeathed the district between the Mersey and the Ribble to the heir of Wilfric, Earl of Mercia.

Prior to the thirteenth century Liverpool was no more than a tiny fishing village that was overshadowed by Chester, Burton and Parkgate on the River Dee. The 'Pool' formed a natural harbour and the main trade passing through the port was salt, which was brought from Cheshire and shipped to Ireland.

In 1207 King John granted Liverpool borough status by Royal Charter and the port developed trade routes to Ireland. Corn, iron, wine and other goods were shipped through Liverpool in the fourteenth century but the Irish trade remained the most important. In one quarter of 1586 sixteen vessels arrived at Liverpool from Ireland with cargoes of yarn and hides and seventeen ships sailed to Ireland with cutlery, soap, textiles and saddles.

Near the end of the Tudor period prosperity in the town increased and friction occurred between Liverpool and Chester. Chester considered the port a mere dependency and claimed the right to control its trade. The dispute was settled in 1658 when the Surveyor General of Customs decided in favour of Liverpool.

In the seventeenth century the port increased its trade with the British colonies. London merchants preferred to ship goods from America to Liverpool and transport them by land to the south of England. In this period Liverpool ship owners carried goods to Africa, slaves to the southern ports of America and sugar, rum and tobacco back to Britain.

In Queen Anne's reign a new dock was planned which was to be the first commercial wet dock in England. Thomas Steer was given the responsibility to survey the ground and provide plans for construction, which included lock gates to retain water levels. It was opened in 1715 but not completed until 1720. However, this dock proved insufficient to deal with the increased trade that was developing. South Dock, later renamed Salthouse Dock, was opened in 1753 and Georges Dock was completed in 1771. Lighthouses were built and dues levied on all vessels were brought under the control of the Dock Trustees appointed by the Town Council.

Commercial traffic increased dramatically during the American War of Independence and Kings, Queens, Princes and Coburg Docks were built. The new Customs House was completed in 1839 and Brunswick Dock was opened in 1832 for the timber trade. Waterloo, Clarence and Victoria Docks were built for the coastal trade. The famous Albert Dock and warehouses were completed in 1846 and were officially opened by Prince Albert.

It was in this period that the Corporation faced the threat of competition from the Harrington Dock Company in Liverpool and a group led by Sir John Tobin and William Laird in Birkenhead. In 1847 the Birkenhead Docks Company was formed and Egerton and Morpeth Docks were opened. The Dock Board took over the Harrington Dock Company in 1843 at a cost of £253,000 and in 1855 Liverpool Corporation purchased the Birkenhead Dock Company.

Over the following years the expansion of the dock system continued but merchants became dissatisfied as they felt that the dues paid to the Corporation were being spent on the town of Liverpool and not on the harbour or the facilities in the docks.

A Royal Commission was appointed in 1853 to investigate the complaints and it recommended that a new body be formed to take over the running of the docks. A Bill was introduced in 1857 and after a long and expensive struggle it was passed in both Houses of Parliament. The Bill created the Mersey Docks & Harbour Board, which would be responsible for all the port accommodation and controlled by twenty-eight Dock Trustees. The first work it undertook was to build Canning Dock for the timber trade and construct the Herculaneum Graving Docks.

In 1873 an Act of Parliament was passed to enable the Board to spend four million pounds to construct Langton, Alexandra and Hornby Docks which created improved facilities for larger vessels. A further three million was spent on deep water berths at Langton and Canada Docks and a new graving dock was built at Canada Dock.

The water was run out of Georges Dock in 1900 for the Mersey Docks & Harbour Board to build their new headquarters accommodation. The Liver Building and Cunard Building were later built to the north of this site.

The 1906 Act of Parliament allowed the Mersey Docks & Harbour Board to construct Gladstone and Gladstone Graving Dock, which was opened by King George V on 11 July 1913. The whole project was completed in 1927 and at that time the system contained the biggest and deepest docks in the world.

The electrification of the dock system was completed in 1925. Electrical energy was supplied at high pressure and distributed for power and lighting purposes. Approximately eighty-one miles of main cable were laid and the Clarence Dock power station, which also generated electricity for parts of Lancashire and Cheshire, supplied power.

Morpeth and Alfred Docks had been built in Birkenhead and the Great Float was completed in 1866. New entrances were built at Alfred Dock and His Royal Highness, the Duke of Edinburgh, opened them on 21 June 1866. Vittoria Dock was constructed and graving docks were completed.

The Liverpool Overhead Railway, which ran between Herculaneum Dock and Alexandra Dock, was opened in 1893. It was an elevated passenger transport system that became known locally as the 'docker's umbrella'. In 1894 it was extended to Seaforth, Waterloo and Dingle in the south of the city. It ran along the Dock Road and gave passengers a view of the docks and vessels moored at the quays.

Land was purchased at Wallasey for oil storage, electrically operated bridges were built and Bidston Dock was completed in 1933. Most quays at Birkenhead were served by an extensive system of railway lines that were connected to a large distribution depot at Morpeth Dock.

The Canadian Pacific Liner Empress Of England (1957/25,585grt) and Shaw Savill cargo vessels in Gladstone Dock.

During the Second World War the whole of the dock system sustained extensive damage, particularly Huskisson and Canada Docks. In 1941 the offices of the Dock Company took a direct hit in an air raid and the top floor and east block burnt out. In the same week the T&J Brocklebank cargo vessel *Malakand*, berthed in Huskisson Dock with a cargo of explosives, caught fire and exploded. The ship and the dock were severely damaged in this action.

The May blitz of 1941 saw the worst period of bombing and damage to the region. Many port facilities were destroyed and required urgent repair to enable the port to function and continue its contribution towards the war effort.

The headquarters of the Battle of the Atlantic was situated in central Liverpool where strategies were devised for defeating the serious U-boat threat to convoys passing through the western approaches.

A total of ninety-one ships were sunk by bombing during the war, 1,285 convoys arrived at the port, seventy-five million tons of cargo and approximately four and three quarters of a million troops passed through the Port.

Following the end of hostilities a massive rebuilding and reconstruction programme was undertaken and the Mersey Docks & Harbour Board had to reassess the changing market trends in goods such as cotton and other traditional cargoes. Riverside Station was built adjacent to the Landing Stage to allow trains to carry passengers directly to the passenger liners and in 1948

Harrison Line cargo vessel Forester (1952/8,377grt) is towed into Langton Lock by tugs of the Liverpool Screw Towing & Lighterage Company.

Atlantic Prelude berthed in Canada Dock, 1972 Atlantic Container Line 11,017grt, 162m x 19m, 17k. She was built as the Montmorency and became Atlantic Prelude in 1978, Incotrains Prelude in 1983 and Atlantic Prelude again in 1985. Renamed Valiant in 1986, Levant Fortune in 1991 and Arion in 1993. She was sold to ship-breakers at Alang where demolition commenced on 8 April 1995.

the world's first port radar station was opened at Gladstone Dock for controlling the shipping traffic within a twenty mile range from the port. The Overhead Railway was in need of substantial investment and consequently was closed down in 1956 depriving the area of a valuable tourist attraction and good transport system.

New berths were constructed and a new dock entrance was completed at Langton Dock in 1962 at a cost of £23 million. In Birkenhead a special iron-ore facility was provided at Bidston Dock for John Summers Steelworks.

The growing oil traffic was catered for by two large projects that were undertaken by the Dock Board. An oil jetty was constructed at the south end of the Liverpool docks system and storage tanks were built on land to the rear of this site. The tremendous increase in this trade forced the Dock Board to build two larger jetties on the Birkenhead side of the river at Tranmere and these were completed in 1960.

In 1964 the Mersey Docks & Harbour Board commissioned a feasibility report on an extension of the docks system, which was prepared by Rendel, Palmer & Tritton, Consulting Engineers, in conjunction with the Board's Engineer in Chief. A survey into the economic factors involved in providing a new dock was authorized by the Board in 1965. The Government sanctioned the plans in 1967 and the contract was awarded to John Howard & Company.

However, in the late sixties the port was subject to various stoppages and industrial disputes. The port workers became very militant during this period and many days were lost because of these stoppages. Ship owners diverted vessels to other ports during these strikes and many found that they could get a more reliable service from the dock workers at these ports. Consequently the trade that had been originally diverted on a temporary basis was lost for good.

The Clan Line berth at Vittoria Dock, Birkenhead.

Blue Star and Clan Line vessels load cargo in Gladstone Dock.

Blue Funnel and Canadian Pacific liners berthed in Gladstone Dock.

The Mersey Docks & Harbour Board heavy lift crane Mammoth (1920/1,524grt) moves a lock gate from Brunswick Dock to drydock to be repaired.

It was also at this time that the container revolution was gaining momentum and other ports had been able to equip themselves with container handling facilities. Liverpool was in danger of being left behind as the new container consortiums quickly became established at London, Felixstowe and Southampton. It was not long before the Port began to feel the loss of this trade and the Mersey Docks & Harbour Board were soon forced into liquidation.

The economic importance of keeping the port open was a prime factor in the Conservative Government's decision to give assistance to the Board. Consequently the Mersey Docks & Harbour Company was established in 1971, which freed the old Board of many of its responsibilities and obligations.

It was in this financial climate that the Seaforth Project was conceived, built and developed. The main purpose of the scheme was to provide deeper docks and longer berths supported by extensive land areas for larger ships and container services with specialized accommodation for packaged timber, bulk grain and installations for the mechanized discharge and handling of meat and other perishable cargoes.

A passage was cut through the north wall of Gladstone Dock to give access to the new dock as ships enter the system through the Gladstone River entrance; it is 1,070ft long and 130ft wide.

The new Seaforth Dock enabled the Port of Liverpool to enter a new phase in its history, allowing the company to provide modern facilities for larger vessels and specialized container ships. It was an acknowledgment and acceptance that containerization as a mode of transport by sea was changing the shipping and transport industries dramatically as it offered benefits such as cargo handling reliability and a fast turn round for shipping companies.

The Grain Terminal berth was designed to accommodate vessels of up to 75,000 tons deadweight and has provision for feeding grain directly to mills on adjacent sites. Alongside the main discharging jetty there is an inlet dock capable of accepting barges and vessels of up to 10,000 tons.

Prior to the commissioning of the container section of the Royal Seaforth Dock vessels used the Gladstone Container Berth, which was provided as a temporary measure. The authority realized that Liverpool was being left behind in the container trade and Gladstone Graving Dock was converted into a wet dock for this traffic. They also built a smaller container berth at Hornby Dock that was used by vessels trading to Spain, Italy and Portugal.

General cargo services were not forgotten as the Mersey Docks & Harbour Company also invested in modernising a number of general cargo berths. The Ocean Steamship Company had its main export terminal at Vittoria Dock in Birkenhead and in collaboration with the Port Authority it built a completely modern set of warehouses and offices. When this work was completed the sheds on the other side of the dock were demolished and a similar terminal was built for the Clan Line. Consequently, the dock became one of the most modern in Europe and it provided facilities for dock workers and transport drivers.

A fruit handling berth was built at Kings Dock for the Aznar Line where perishable goods were unloaded by conveyor belts directly to vehicles. Unfortunately this berth had a very short life, as it was part of the ill-fated South Docks system which was closed to traffic in 1972-1973. Originally it was hoped that the berth, incorporating sheds and cranes, could be uplifted and transferred in sections to the Aznar Line's new berth in the Alexandra Dock. The plan proved to be too expensive and consequently it was shelved.

Up to 1972 there were five passenger liners regularly sailing in and out of the Port. The *Empress of Canada* sailed between Liverpool and Quebec until early in 1972 when she was sold to an American company to cruise out of Miami. Elder Dempster Line's *Aureol* sailed from Liverpool every month on a regular service to West Africa but she was transferred to the Port of Southampton in a rationalization of service. In 1970 an experimental service was started by the Shaw Savill Line with their passenger vessel *Southern Cross*. They wanted to test the market to see if there were sufficient people in the north west of England who would support a cruise vessel sailing from Liverpool. The company also provided cruises in 1971 but declined to accept

Prometheus (1967/12,094grt) loads at the Blue Funnel berth at Vittoria Dock, Birkenhead.

A busy day at Princes Landing Stage in 1961.

the Dock Company's offer of a berth inside the dock system following the closure of the Liverpool Landing Stage.

The Princes and Georges Landing Stages formed a continuous structure, 2,534ft long by eighty feet wide, which was carried on approximately 200 pontoons. There were ten bridges connecting with the shore and a floating roadway that gave access to private and commercial vehicles. Originally the Board planned to scrap the structure but this would have meant the closure of the local ferry services and there would have been no suitable berths for the ships of the Isle of Man Steam Packet Company. Following discussions with the Merseyside Passenger Transport Executive and the Isle of Man Government it was decided to build a smaller structure which would accommodate the Manx and Mersey ferries.

Special berths were built for the Belfast Steamship Company in West Princes Dock and the British & Irish Line in Trafalgar Dock to provide modern facilities for the new roll-on/roll-off passenger ferries that were being introduced on the Belfast and Dublin routes.

It was claimed that the United Kingdom's entry into the Common Market would mean that Liverpool would become the 'Gateway to Europe' for goods shipped from North American and Canadian ports. Containers could be shipped directly on to rail wagons and

19

A Dock Board dredger carries out work at the entrance to the Gladstone river entrance.

Port Line vessel Port Caroline (1968/12,398grt) is painted by her crew prior to loading cargo. In 1982 she was tranferred to T&J Brocklebank and renamed Matra. In 1983 she was renamed Golden Dolphin and was broken up at Shanghai in 1985.

Apapa (1948/11,651grt) and Aureol (1951/14,083grt) at the Elder Dempster berth in Brocklebank Dock.

then trans-shipped to their final destination after a short voyage from an East Coast port. It was hoped, therefore, that the capital invested in the Container Terminal would pay dividends if this additional traffic was shipped through the port.

In 1971 over nineteen million people lived within 100 miles of Liverpool. This was four million more than the total population of Australia and New Zealand and two million more than the combined population of Norway, Sweden and Denmark. Four of Britain's major conurbations fall within the 100 mile radius as were seventy-two towns or urban areas with a population each exceeding 50,000 together containing ten million people. The North West was the second largest region after the South East in terms of working population and 45.6 per cent of workers were employed in manufacturing compared with a national average of 38.6 per cent. Within the 100-mile radius of Liverpool there were:

59.4% of all metal, engineering and shipbuilding firms.
58.9% of all textile, leather and clothing manufacturers.
51.2% of all manufacturers.
46.2% of all food, drink and tobacco firms.
43.6% of all chemical and allied industries.
36.2% of all paper and printing industries.

Only 30% of the population of the United Kingdom lived within 100 miles radius in 1971 but the following goods were purchased by this group:

53% of all branded goods.
49% of all cigarettes and tobacco.
47% of all domestic electrical appliances.
47% of all items of men's clothing.

In 1971 14,320 vessels used the Port of Liverpool with a combined net registered tonnage of 29,906,893 tons as shown below:

Foreign (excluding petroleum) 7,153,000
Foreign 3,998,000
Coastwise (excluding petroleum) 634,000
Coastwise 590,000
Foreign (Petroleum) 15,099,000
Coastwise 2,512,000

Lady of Mann (1930/3,104grt) passes a Clan liner in Alfred Dock, Birkenhead.

The new Liverpool to Belfast car ferry Ulster Prince (1967/4,270grt) at the Belfast Steamship berth in Princes Dock.

Mersey Ferries Royal Daffodil (1962/468grt) on a sailing from Liverpool to Seacombe. She was built as the Overchurch and was renamed in 1999.

A rough winter's day at Fort Perch Rock at the entrance to the River Mersey.

Two
Seaforth

Zim and Atlantic Container Line vessels load cargo at the Royal Seaforth Container terminal.

In the years following the opening of the Royal Seaforth Dock the Port of Liverpool has changed dramatically. The South Docks System was closed in 1972-1973 as it was generally outdated having high dredging and operating costs and that the traffic they handled could be absorbed elsewhere in the port.

By 1982 the amount of cargo passing through the port had fallen to 9.3 million tonnes because of a very bad industrial relations record and also as a consequence of Britain's entry into the European Common Market. The Dock Authority embarked on a major reorganization and drastic changes in working practices. In 1984 this started to improve their financial condition and a profit of £800,000 was made on a turnover of nine million tons of cargo.

Birkenhead Docks now only has two or three active berths for deep sea cargo vessels and is home to various preserved warships and other vessels laid-up and out of service.

However, in 1999, containers shipped through the Port rose to a new record of 515,000 compared to 487,000 in 1998, putting Liverpool in the top ten North European ports. Traffic in 1999 totaled 28,863,000 tonnes and the Royal Seaforth Container Terminal attracted twelve new services between 1990 and 1994. The Forest Products Terminal at Seaforth attracted three new services in 1994 from Canada, South Africa and Brazil. Daily roll-on/roll-off and lift-on/lift-off services to Belfast and Dublin handle more than three million tonnes of trade each year which amounts to 30% of all freight crossing the Irish Sea. It is the only British

Tropean (1980/14,375grt) turns in the River Mersey off New Brighton prior to docking at Canada Dock to load scrap metal.

26

Sibotura (1992/41,189grt) unloads coal at the Powergen berth at Gladstone Dock.

port in the Irish Sea that serves both Northern and Southern Ireland moving 60% of all unitized traffic between the Republic and the United Kingdom.

A designated Channel Tunnel Euro Rail Terminal for unitized cargo has been established to provide a land bridge for trade to and from Ireland, the United Kingdom and Europe via the Chunnel. This terminal now offers daily services to Italy, Spain, Switzerland, Germany, France, and Luxembourg for coastal and deep-sea shipping services. This acquisition followed the company move into shipping line operation when it took over the Coastal Container Line in 1991.

The Port is now handling a similar annual tonnage of cargo as in 1971 when over 14,000 port operations workers were employed to discharge and load the cargoes. Today approximately 600 people are employed in the Port.

Liverpool still has trading links with practically every port in the world. It is the major United Kingdom port for trade with the Eastern Seaboard of North America. The Port imports more grain than any other United Kingdom port, exports over 1 million tonnes of scrap metal a year and is one of the major United Kingdom ports for timber and forest products and edible oils and fats.

PowerGen has developed a new £40 million environmentally sensitive bulk terminal at Gladstone Dock. It has the capacity to handle up to six million tonnes of coal a year, mainly for outward rail movement to Fiddlers Ferry Power Station.

The Mersey Docks & Harbour Company has a number of property developments including the Liverpool Freeport Park, which includes their new headquarters, and others at Stanley Dock, Waterloo Dock and Warehouses, Princes Dock and Woodside Business Park in Birkenhead.

27

World Lapis (1981/16,250grt) unloads animal feed at Canada Dock.

It is a major creator of employment in the area generating between 49,000 and 105,000 jobs on Merseyside, which is 9-19½% of the regions total employment. The Port creates 125,000 to 311,000 jobs throughout the United Kingdom and additional trade through the Port generated by the Company's proposed capital expenditure programme for 1992-1998 is expected to create another 9,000 to 23,000 jobs in the region and 29,000 to 76,000 across the United Kingdom.

The Company owns 2,000 acres (809 hectares) of dockland at Liverpool and Birkenhead. It is responsible for maintaining the channels and approaches to the Mersey. The Dock Estate is included in a region that has been granted European Union Objective One Status enabling projects to qualify for grants of up to 75%.

A new £2 million development at Canada Dock has recently been completed. This is a 65,000 cubic metre bulk terminal and store for animal feed. Two dual-purpose buildings were completed alongside the West Float in Birkenhead in 1994 as Phase 2 of a Bulk Industrial Zone development of the Liverpool Freeport.

Early in 1995 planning applications were submitted to Sefton Council for the partial closure of the Dock Road and the expansion of the Port and Freeport to create a site of more than seventy acres with 80,000 square metres of warehousing and industrial space. This project is expected to create over 500 jobs. Work began on this development in 1997 when a mile long section of the Dock Road was closed to traffic and seventy acres of land to the east was enclosed within the Port and Liverpool Freeport boundary.

In conjunction with the David MacLean Group, the Mersey Docks & Harbour Company are redeveloping an area around Princes Dock. The plans include office accommodation, residential flats and a hotel with a conference centre. The warehouse at Waterloo Dock is also being converted into 400 luxury apartments in a joint project with Barratts the builders.

Outline planning permission has been applied to develop seventy acres of dockland to the north of Waterloo Dock. This would incorporate residential property, leisure facilities including a marina and commercial development.

Elm (1984/13,019grt) is assisted by Cory tugs in Gladstone Dock as Wadi Al Kamar (1985/27,589grt) loads scrap metal.

Sail Training vessel Lord Nelson berthed at Seacombe Landing Stage.

Shipping Corporation of India vessel State of Tripura (1978/14,166grt) at Cavendish Quay in the Birkenhead Dock system.

Three
Liners

Direct Lines Apollon (1961/28,574grt) docks in Liverpool at the end of a Mediterranean cruise in 1998. She was broken up at Alang in 2004.

Canadian Pacific Empress of England cruise itineraries for 1970.

Empress of England

Itineraries

Empress of England
Departing from Liverpool

20th December 1969-6th January 1970
Christmas & New Year Cruise to Las Palmas, St. Vincent (C.V.I.), Madeira, Lisbon.
Fares from £120. U.S. $288.

6th January-13th February West Indies & Rio
Cruise to Las Palmas, Freetown, Rio de Janeiro, Trinidad, Tortola, San Juan, Madeira.
Fares from £350. U.S. $840.

14th February-6th March Valentine Cruise to Tenerife, St. Vincent (C.V.I.) Dakar, Madeira Cadiz, Lisbon. Fares from £145. U.S. $348.

6th March-26th March Sunshine Isles Cruise to Ponta del Gada, St. Vincent (C.V.I.) Madeira, Las Palmas, Casablanca, Lisbon.
Fares from £145. U.S. $348.

26th March-31st March Easter Cruise to Coruna
Fares from £45. U.S. $108.

18th July-1st August Cruise to Lyse Fjord to view Pulpit Rock, Copenhagen, Leningrad, Stockholm and Hamburg. Fares from £125. U.S. $300.

20th November-1st December Cruise to Tenerife, Madeira, Casablanca, Gibraltar.
Fares from £100. U.S. $240.

21st December 1970 - 6th January 1971
Cruise to Casablanca, Dakar, Madeira, Lisbon. Fares to be announced later.

Offices:

London: Trafalgar Square, W.C.2.
Telephone 01-930 6601

Glasgow: 159/161 St. Vincent Street
Telephone 041-221 9982

Liverpool: Royal Liver Building, Pier Head
Telephone 051-236 5690

Montreal: Windsor Station
Telephone 861-6511

New York: 581 Fifth Avenue
Telephone 769-4433

Even the large passenger liners are returning to the River Mersey. Representatives of the Port attended the Seatrade Cruise Shipping Exhibition in Miami and the Port of Liverpool are active members of Cruise European organization promoting United Kingdom and European ports to cruise companies. CTC Cruise Lines commenced using Liverpool as a cruise port in 1992 and the Royal Caribbean Line vessels *Sun Viking*, 18,455 gross tons, and *Song of Norway*, 22,945 gross tonnage, have visited the port.

Cunard Line's vessel *Crown Dynasty*, 19,089 gross tons, berthed at Princes Landing Stage in 1993 and the company's flagship, *Queen Elizabeth 2*, called at Liverpool in 1994 as part of her silver jubilee celebrations. She had made her first visit to Liverpool several years earlier

In the summer of 1997 Direct Holidays announced that they would be operating a programme of cruises from Liverpool in 1998. The statement added that they would be using the *Edinburgh Castle*, of 32,753 gross tons, which was previously the Italian liner *Eugenio Costa*, on cruises to the Mediterranean, Atlantic Islands, Iceland, Greenland and the Norwegian Fjords.

Direct Holidays were one of Britains' largest direct sell companies and were backed by the Royal Bank of Scotland with full membership of the Association of British Travel Agents and licenced by the Civil Aviation Authority. As their products were sold direct to the public they were able to offer their cruises at very competitive prices and, consequently, were able to pass on the savings to the customer. Direct Cruises were following the success of C.T.C. Lines *Southern Cross*, 17,042 gross tons, which had been operating out of Liverpool on similar cruises.

Queen Elizabeth 2 (1968/70,327grt) arrives in the river on a round Britain cruise.

The announcement by Direct was a tremendous boost to the Port and many wished success to them in this new venture. It was quickly followed by another giving details of a second vessel which was to cruise alongside the *Edinburgh Castle* from Liverpool, Greenock and Newcastle. This was the *Apollo*, 28,574 gross tons, which was launched as the *Empress of Canada* for Canadian Pacific and sailed on her maiden voyage from Liverpool on 24 April 1961. However, various problems occurred with both vessels and the line was forced to cancel several of the advertised cruises from the 1998 programme.

In the summer of 1998 it was announced that Airtours had acquired Direct Cruises and that the new owners were committed to providing cruises in 1999 from Greenock, Leith, Liverpool and Belfast. The programme of cruises for 2000 covered the period from April to October with the *Apollo* making a number of sailings from Liverpool. However, it was announced in 1999 that the cruise programme from British ports would not operate in the year 2000.

By 1999 the cruise liners should have been able to berth again at Liverpool Landing Stage as the depth of water was to be increased by a dredging programme and a new passenger terminal was also to be provided which would handle 500,000 cruise and Irish Sea passengers. However, an adverse decision of the Court stopped the proposed development of the site at the Pier Head and some traffic was lost on the Manx route. The Dock Company and the operator, Sea Containers, are now examining alternative ways of providing the facilities necessary for the retention and future development of the Isle of Man and Dublin services.

The intensive dredging programme was undertaken at the end of 1999 that enabled the Cunard liner *Caronia* to berth at the Landing Stage to be renamed by the Deputy Prime Minister, John Prescott on 10 December 1999. She had originally been called *Vistafjord*.

Astra 1 (19655/5,535grt) She was built as the Istra, became Astra in 1991 and Astra 1 in 1996. In 1999 she was renamed Nautilus, and Arion in 2000.

Caronia (1973/24,492grt) swings in the river prior to berthing at the Princes Landing Stage. She became Saga Ruby in 2005.

Port of Liverpool Statistics

	2003	2004
Containers	578	616
Forest products	391	295
Grain and animal feed	2,377	2,289
Bulk liquids	727	774
Other bulks	6,296	6,051
Oil terminal	11,406	11,406
General cargo	556	374
Ro-ro (1,000s of units)	467	513
Passengers (1,000s)	734	720
Total throughput	31,753	32,171

(All figures are in kteu – kilotonne equivalent units – unless otherwise stated)

Stena Line Koningin Beatrix (1986/22,289grt) arrives for her annual overhaul at Cammell Laird shipyard.

Four

Coastal and Supply Services

Merchant Ferries Dawn Merchant (1998/22,046grt) sails to Dublin. She was sold in 2005 and renamed Europax Appia.

Coastal Container Line Coastal Sound (1983/1,876grt) loads at the Royal Seaforth Container Terminal.

In 1993 the M.D. & H.B. Company's floating crane, Mammoth, was chartered by her builders to carry out a construction project in Denmark. The Mammoth took seven and a half days to sail around Lands End and through the English Channel to the port of Kalundborg. The Mammoth has also assisted in the installation of lock gates at Bristol's Royal Portbury Dock and link spans in the Orkney Islands of Westray and Sanday.

The Company acquired a fifty per cent interest in Merchant Ferries Ltd in 1993. Merchant Ferries operated daily roll-on/roll-off services between Heysham, Fleetwood and Warrenport. The arrangement also involved a fifty per cent interest in Merchant Ferries freight forwarding company M.T.S. Shipping and a twenty year agreement with Belfast Harbour Commissioners to operate at the port's Victoria Terminal. This acquisition followed the company's move into shipping line operation when it took over the Coastal Container Line in 1991.

Another acquisition, in 1993, was the agreement to pay £103 million for Medway Ports Ltd, who operate the Port of Sheerness. The Company stated that the acquisition of the Medway Ports would broaden their geographical base as it is a deep-water port and there are no tidal restrictions. It is one of the leading import ports for fruit, cars and forestry products and a ferry service operates to Holland. Medway Ports also held freehold and leasehold interests in the former Royal Naval Dockyard at Chatham.

The summer of 1995 also saw an extension of the Coastal Container Lines services when a weekly triangular container service was provided between Belfast, Greenock and the Liverpool Royal Seaforth Container Terminal. The line also continues to operate between Liverpool and Belfast, Dublin and from Cardiff to Dublin and Belfast.

38

In 1996 the Mersey Docks & Harbour Company acquired BG Freight Line, the Rotterdam-based deep sea feeder and continental door-to-door cargo carrier which serves Dublin, Belfast, Cork, Rotterdam and Antwerp.

A new passenger/cargo service between Liverpool and Dublin commenced in January 1999 with two new vessels *Dawn Merchant* and *Brave Merchant*, both of 22,046 gross tonnes.

In April 1995 Eurolink Ferries introduced a new service between Sheerness and Vlissingen in Holland with two chartered vessels which were renamed *Euromantique* and *Euromagique*. Each vessel carried 500 passengers, cars, commercial vehicles and coaches on the seven-hour day and nine-hour night crossing. However, it was announced that the service was to close in 1997 and the last sailing took place on 1 December 1997. The vessels were then offered for charter.

Following the announcement of a 61 per cent increase in profits for 1994 the Company invested over £5 million at Sheerness by improvements to temperature controlled stores for fresh produce warehousing for forest products and land expansion. A ten-year contract with Volkswagen-Audi, and a decision by Hyundai to move 15,000 vehicles a year through the Port, was greeted as a positive step in the development of Sheerness.

The concept of Liverpool becoming a 'Land Bridge' between Ireland and the rest of Europe became a reality in March 1994 when the first train from the Euro-Rail Terminal at Seaforth travelled via the Channel Tunnel. Journey times from Liverpool to Brussels and Paris are fifteen hours, Bordeaux twenty-nine hours, Milan thirty-six hours and Stuttgart twenty-eight hours.

Acila 1982, Shell Tanker, 8,806grt, 141m x 21m, 14k. She was built as the Shelltrans and was renamed in 1994.

39

In 1994 Hamilton Oil Company chose the Port of Liverpool as their Liverpool Bay operational base. The contract was won against strong competition from other ports in the region including Mostyn Docks in North Wales. Hamilton Oil operated from berths at West Hornby and Alexandra Docks and oil and gas from Liverpool Bay is pumped to the storage base at the Point of Ayr on the North-Wales coast.

On 25 May 1995 the Lord Mayor of Liverpool opened a new passenger terminal for the Isle of Man Steam Packet Company at Liverpool Landing Stage. The terminal provides seating, an automatic baggage reclaim carousel and a new booking office.

The Mersey Docks & Harbour Company announced plans in 1995 to construct a £16.5 million roll-on/roll-off river berth for vessels involved in the Irish Sea trade. The terminal would allow vessels to load and discharge in the river, saving time in locking in and out of the dock system. It was envisaged that two vessels would be able to berth at the new floating stage, which was expected to deal with six ships a day when it became operational in the year 2000. Work started on filling in Trafalgar Dock to provide the main storage, parking, marshalling and office spaces. The old British & Irish passenger terminal on the site was to be refurbished to cater for foot passengers. However, it was announced in 1999 that the river berth would not now be located at this site and that a feasibility project was being completed on providing the berths off Langton Dock.

Gulf Offshore Lines Clwyd Supporter (1984/2,767grt) sails to service the gas rigs in the Liverpool Bay area.

40

The former Royal yacht Libertatea/Nahlin (1930/1,391grt) in Clarence Graving Dock. She was towed to Hamburg by the heavy lift vessel Condock V on 27 July 2005.

Supply vessels are berthed at A.S. Co. UK's quay at West Hornby Dock where materials and equipment are loaded for the Liverpool Bay platforms.

By 1997 the Liverpool Bay Development partnership had invested over £1.1 billion in four Irish Sea gas and oil fields. B.H.P. Petroleum reached production rates of 300 million cubic feet (8.49 million cubic metres) and 70,000 barrels of oil each day. Flights to service the fields were provided by Bond Helicopters from Liverpool Airport, whose distinctive red craft were a familiar site on their flight path down the centre of the River Mersey.

A new bulk terminal and store for animal feed received its first ship in the autumn of 1994. The berth at South West 1 Canada Dock is able to discharge cargo by crane into mobile receiving hoppers and a conveyor system into the storage shed.

Together with the Twelve Quays site at Birkenhead the two double river berths would handle a combined total in excess of half a million units a year. Twelve Quays was taken over from Forth Ports in 1997 and in 1999 tender documents were issued and construction work was due to commence in the final quarter of the year 2001.

The projects give an indication of how valuably the Company views the increasing Irish Sea coastal traffic business and how determined they are to provide up-to-date facilities for shippers, hauliers and ship operators.

A major operator in the Irish Sea trade introduced a new significant ship into their Liverpool to Belfast service in 1995. The *Norse Mersey* was built in Italy for Norse Irish Ferries, which began operating from Liverpool shortly after Stena Sealink withdrew from this service.

In 1997 the line introduced two new purpose-built vessels to this service. The ships were named *Mersey Viking* and *Lagan Viking*, 21,500 gross tonnes, which have a 330-passenger capacity, 2,300 metre of trailer lanes and a service speed of twenty-two knots. The increased speed of these vessels allows them to cut an hour off the sailing time and early in the summer of 1998 the company introduced daytime sailings on this route. In 1999 it was announced that this Line was to be taken over by Merchant Ferries who had planned to open a Liverpool to Belfast service with two new purpose-built vessels of similar design to their other two ships.

The Royal Seaforth Terminal was at the centre of a serious industrial dispute in 1995 when 329 port workers took unofficial action following the dismissal of eighty men from an independent stevedoring company. When the men refused to cross an unofficial picket line the company dismissed them and recruited a new work force. Within two months the Terminal was operating again with the new workers and the Company claimed substantial improvements both in productivity and efficiency. The largest container ships are turned around in twelve hours and bulk carriers are discharged at a rate of 20,000 tonnes a day with Panamax sized vessels unloading in three and a half days. The unofficial dispute lasted for twenty-eight months before the 327 dock workers accepted an offer from the Mersey Docks & Harbour Company. It was estimated that the total cost of the settlement would be in the region of £10 million and by the year 2000 the new workforce had increased productivity by fifty per cent.

Early in 1998 P&O European Ferries demonstrated their confidence in the Port of Liverpool by signing a twelve-year contract to use the Port. The company operates daily roll-on/roll-off ferries from Dublin to their berth at Gladstone Dock but will move to the new river berths when they are operational.

In 1999 P&O announced that they had placed an order for a new vessel for this route which cost Euro fifty million and will replace the *European Leader* which was transferred to their Fleetwood to Larne route. The new *European Ambassador* has a service speed of twenty-five knots, reducing the passage time from eight to six hours. There is more than 2,000 lane metres on the vehicle deck and

British & Irish Lines first container vessel Tipperary (1969/622grt) off the Waterloo River Entrance on a voyage to Dublin.

Manxman (1955/2,495grt) berthed at Wallasey Landing Stage which has since been demolished. It is the site of the Twelve Quays river berths which were opened in 2002 and are operated by Norse Merchant Ferries.

Ben My Chree (1998/12,504grt) on berthing trails in the River Mersey in 1998.

drive through facilities are provided. Accommodation for 405 passengers is provided in eighty-two cabins with 222 berths and also the provision of seventy-four Pullman seats.

In 1996 the Isle of Man Steam Packet Company operated 200 sailings into the Port of Liverpool and in 1997 there were 300 sailings in the summer season and another 200 in the spring and autumn. The introduction of the new Superseacat service by the parent company, Seacontainers, has proved very successful and has exceeded all expectations. The Mersey Docks & Harbour Company is developing an area to the north of the Pier Head to provide improved facilities for passengers and cars using the Douglas and Dublin services. A floating platform was attached to the end of the landing stage on 18 August 2000 to provide additional accommodation for staff and passengers using these services.

In 1996 the Mersey Docks & Harbour Company was ranked two hundred and fifty-third in the Financial Times Top 500 United Kingdom companies, against 306 in 1995. It now claims to operate Britain's largest and most successful Freeport, which handles £1 million worth of goods a day.

Since opening in November 1984, Liverpool Freeport has handled £2.5 billion worth of traffic. It has Britain's first operational freight village located alongside the designated Euro-Rail Terminal for Channel Tunnel freight and offers exemption from Import Duty, VAT, EU levies and quotas.

Norse Merchant Ferries Mersey Viking (1997/21,500grt) reverses into her berth in Brocklebank Dock. She became Dublin Viking in 2005 when she was transferred to the Birkenhead–Dublin service.

Cory Towage tug Norton Cross (1985/189grt) moves a vessel into Alfred Dock, Birkenhead.

Howard Smith tugs assist a vessel in Langton Dock.

P&O European ferry European Leader (1975/10,987grt) prepares to sail to Dublin. She was sold to the Stena Line in 2004 and was renamed Stena Leader.

Seacat Isle of Man (1991/3,003grt) passes Superseacat Three (1999/4,700grt) off Gladstone Dock.

Lady of Mann (1976/4,482grt) leaves Liverpool Landing Stage on a voyage to Douglas, Isle of Man. She was sold in 2005, renamed Panagia Soumela, and converted to a stern loader car ferry.

King Orry (1975/7,555grt) undertakes her annual overhaul in Bidston Graving Dock at Birkenhead. Sold by the Isle of Man Steam Packet in 1998, becoming Moby Love.

Vessels laid up in Sandon Dock in 1999.

The Mersey Docks & Harbour Company dredger Mersey Mariner (1981/2,191grt) works in Canada Dock.

Five

Present and Future

HMS Plymouth and HMS Onyx owned by the Historic Warship Trust are open to the public in the East Float, Birkenhead.

Productivity and safety is being increased at the Royal Seaforth Container Terminal by the provision of a new logistics centre to provide documentation clearance facilities as well as on site accommodation for shipping lines, agents and H.M. Customs & Excise.

There will be space for thirty per cent more containers at a terminal designed to turn around road transport even faster and more efficiently while providing a safer working environment by minimizing the number of vehicles and people and the areas to which they have access.

On 1 January 1997 Stanton Grove, a major United Kingdom products distribution company, took over control of the Royal Seaforth Forest Products Terminal. This enabled the Port of Liverpool to provide a fully integrated terminal to customers, which was operated by a skilled organization with high-calibre staff.

Stanton Grove's customers include a monthly Gearbulk West Canadian service discharging paper reels and lumber, the Diana Shipping East Canadian lumber service, Panocean's call with Far East hardwood and imports of Latavian timber. Over 200,000 tonnes of timber and 150,000 tonnes of paper products were handled in 1997.

In 1997 the Royal Seaforth Grain Terminal again exceeded the previous years tonnage handling in excess of 1.3 million tonnes.

United Storage now offers a total capacity of 287,000 cubic metres of storage space at the Port. They provide 144,000 cubic metres of tank storage at its Canada and Gladstone Docks and 152,630 cubic metres at its East Lewis Quay site in Birkenhead. The company stores and distributes all kinds of bulk liquids including vegetable oils, molasses, industrial chemicals and lubrication oils.

Shell's Tranmere Oil Terminal now has two specially converted crude oil storage tanks each offering a capacity of 30,000 tonnes and costing a total of £1 million. These are used for crude oil imported from the Fionavon Field off the west coast of Scotland.

CMA CGM Cezanne (1998/26,131 grt) leaves the Royal Seaforth Container Terminal with a cargo of empty containers.

John Harker vessel Deepdale H (1965/385grt) passes under Duke Street bridge in the Birkenhead dock system.

New warehouses are constructed at Cavendish Quay, Birkenhead in 2001.

In 1997 Fastbulk handled in excess of 140,000 tonnes at South Alexandra Dock. Fastbulk specialize in cargoes of grain, animal feed commodities, woodchip, lead, manganese ore and ferrous chrome. They have been operating at Liverpool for over ten years and have two warehouses in the Liverpool Freeport providing 90,000 square metres of capacity.

Backhouse Bloore Limited offers a complete logistics service moving more than two million tonnes of cargo each year. This is discharged via a 250 metre long conveyor link from the S10 Berth at the Royal Seaforth Dock to a 'quarry' at the rate of up to 4,000 tonnes an hour. Volclay handle 80,000 tonnes of bentonite and other material at their Birkenhead site. The bentonite is sieved to similar size granules or milled into powder form.

C.E.T.C.O. was established in Birkenhead in 1996 and exports sixty – seventy per cent of its concrete waterproofing products, which are used in the construction industry. There are plans to expand their facility in the near future.

Refrigerators, old cars, steel cans and other items are recycled by European Metal Recycling Ltd, who operate from seven berths at the port and have installed a £250,000 railhead at Alexandra Dock. S. Norton & Company also completed a £4 million resurfacing and upgrading project at South No.2 Canada Branch Dock.

The Chilean shipping line, Compania Chilena de Navegacion Interoceanica S.A. (C.C.N.I.), has a joint operation with various shipping lines. C.C.N.I. operate a fleet of container-bulkers between the west coast of South America and Europe calling at the Royal Seaforth Container Terminal once a month.

Oceanic Cargo Lines, which began operating from the port in 1995, provides a service from Lagos in Nigeria and other West African Ports. The line carries both conventional cargo and

CCNI Angol (1998/28,148grt) arrives in the Mersey from South America.

A new propeller is loaded onto a coaster by the Mersey Docks & Harbour Company floating crane Mersey Mammoth (1986/1,793grt).

containers and uses a berth at Canada Dock with sailings every six weeks. In 1997 Oceanic Cargo Lines Business increased by twenty-five per cent and they are hoping to increase their sailing frequency in the near future.

Portuguese granite imports, which are carried by Sontrade Lines, have doubled during 1997. Sontrade specialize in various general cargo products and have established their own stevedoring operation at Huskisson Dock and are offering this facility to other users of the port.

Breakbulk, heavylifts, steel, timber, containers and general cargo are handled by Danback at North 2 and South 3 Canada Branch Docks. Birkenhead Stevedoring is a joint venture between the Mersey Docks & Harbour Company, Stanton Grove and C. Shaw Lovell & Sons and specialize in steel and forest product cargoes.

The Warrant Group, Stone Manganese Marine and Henry Bath and Sons are three examples of companies that traded successfully in 1997-1998 and are committed to maintaining a presence in the Port of Liverpool in the future.

A major project called the Liverpool Intermodal Freeport Terminal (L.I.F.T.) costing £20 million of private and public investment is extending the dock estate and Free Zone by seventy acres and creating 860,000 square feet (79,894 square metres) by the year 2003. The project is situated within the boundaries of the Liverpool Freeport and is rail linked.

Freeport Warehousing intend to transfer from Alexandra Dock and will offer an internal container bay. Freeport is fifty per cent owned by the Mersey Docks & Harbour Company.

Duty Free Warehouse, the R.H. Group, Sanchez (UK) Ltd, Express Cargo Forwarding, S.F.K.

53

Milenaki (1970/16,153grt) arrives at the port in 1999 with a cargo of cement from Italy.

P&O European Ferries Pride of Rathlin (1973/12,503grt) in dry dock at Cammell Laird's yard at Birkenhead. In 2000 she became BSP 111 and left Larne, Co. Antrim, on 13 November that year for service in Indonesia.

and Huttons International are all based at the Liverpool Freeport providing a vast variety of warehousing, forwarding, distribution, groupage, bonded warehousing and transport facilities.

In 1999 two new ship-to-shore gantry cranes were ordered for the Royal Seaforth Container Terminal as part of a £12 million redevelopment programme. Nearly 300,000 sq.ft of warehousing and light industrial units have been developed at Liverpool Intermodal Freeport Terminal and construction of another 150,000 sq.ft is proposed. At Princes Dock the first office buildings were occupied and a new 4 star Crowne Plaza hotel was opened in 1998.

A new sixteen metre pilot launch was delivered from Sweden in 1999 and a contract was placed with Cory Towage for the provision of a purpose-built oil spill recovery vessel in compliance with new Government regulations.

The *Mersey Mammoth* undertook contract work at Hinkley Point on the Bristol Channel, Falmouth, Stornoway, Glasgow, Barrow, Newport, Swansea, Belfast and Douglas, Isle of Man.

A joint venture concession in Argentina began in 1998 and contracts were signed for the development and operation of a US $32 million bulk grain and fertilizer terminal at the Port of Mombasa in Kenya. A consortium led by the Company was declared preferred bidder for the privatization of the Port of Maputo, Mozambique.

Six wind turbines were constructed on the seawall at Seaforth. They began generating electricity for sale to the National Grid in 1999.

Early in 2000 the Dock Company acquired Concorde Container Line which serves continental Europe and the East Coast of England and Scotland.

The Mersey Docks & Harbour Company is clearly looking to the future and is diversifying into a range of wholly and part-owned subsidiary and joint venture companies including shipping services, ship owning and stevedoring. It is also Britain's largest port management consultancy with projects in China, Kenya, Australia, Russia, Abu Dhabi and Cyprus.

In 2000 the Port of Liverpool was ranked fourth among United Kingdom container ports serving the North Atlantic trades. By 2005 it handled more container trade with the United States of America and Canada than any other port in the country. Other developments in the global container market have opened up new routes for shippers moving goods through the Seaforth Terminal.

The Mersey Docks and Harbour Company are also developing a river terminal off Gladstone Dock which will be capable of handling the new generation of larger post-Panamax vessels. An application for a Harbour Revision Order was submitted in 2005 with a view to the £80 million development being completed by 2008.

The new terminal will be capable of handling two of the new generation of larger container ships on its 800m-long quay and the 17 hectare terminal will almost double Liverpool's container capacity.

At the end of 2005 Norse Merchant introduced two new vessels on their service to Belfast from the Twelve Quays terminal and transferred *Dublin Viking* and *Liverpool Viking* to the Dublin route.

On 22 September 2005, the Port of Liverpool changed ownership when the parent company, the Mersey Docks and Harbour Company, was acquired by the leading property and transport group, Peel Holdings Ltd. The Peel Group's ports division now becomes the second largest ports group in the United Kingdom, incorporating Clydeport, the Manchester Ship Canal, Heysham port and Medway Ports. It also now operates container terminals in Cardiff and the Irish ports of Belfast and Dublin.

Merseyside Passenger Transport leaflet advertising Royal Iris Cruises from New Brighton, Seacombe and Liverpool in June, 1971.

The Ocean Youth Club yacht Greater Manchester Challenge passes the wind generators at the entrance to the river.

A view of the various small vessels owned by the Merseyside Maritime Museum berthed at Albert Dock.

Blue Nile (1980/9,140grt) docks in the West Float at Birkenhead.

Co-op Travel

Special cruise along the full length of the

MANCHESTER SHIP CANAL

aboard the T.S.M.V. 'Egremont'
Saturday, 13th May, 1972

TIME TABLE

Saturday, 13th May

08-30 hours. Embarkation commences in T.S.M.V. 'Egre... Pomona Docks—Cornbrook Road entrance, off C... Road, Manchester.

09-00 hours. On completion of embarkation, T.S.M.V. ...mont' leaves for New Brighton via the Manchester... Canal and Mersey Estuary. (Please see map and his... note.)

16-00 hours (approx.). Due to arrive Liverpool

There is a frequent service of trains from Liverpool (Lime S... Station) to Manchester, and the following are considered to ... most suitable, but passengers may return by any train they ...

Liverpool depart	17-05	17-35	18-10	18-35	19-35
Piccadilly arrive	—	18-29	—	19-26	20-27
Victoria arrive	17-47	—	18-56	—	—

A BUFFET will be available in the T.S.M.V. 'Egremont' during the ... for the sale of light refreshments.

Issued by Co-op Travel
Corporation Street, Manchester, M60 4ES

CWS Printers Manchester

T.S.M.V. Egremont Manchester Ship Canal cruise details for Saturday 13 May 1972.

Regular Direct Outward Services

1971

Shipping Line Index

Country	Key Number
Aden	3, 14, 19, 20, 38, 39, 41
Albania	29
Algeria	24, 29, 53, 65
Angola	20, 28, 36, 38, 39, 64
Argentina	30, 44, 47
Ascension Island	20
Australia	1, 26
Bahrain	4, 46, 76
Belgium	43, 52
Bermuda	62
Brazil	2, 13, 47, 48
British Honduras	39
Bulgaria	29, 53, 55, 65
Burma	8, 41, 81
Cameroon	9, 28, 36, 42, 58, 64
Canada – Atlantic	16, 33, 40, 60
– Pacific	11, 27
– Great Lakes	16, 40, 60
Canary Islands	7, 9, 20, 28, 36, 38, 64
Cape Verde Islands	75
Ceylon	8, 20
Chile	22, 23, 62
China	10, 17, 18
Colombia	22, 39, 62
Congo	9, 28, 36, 64
Cyprus	29, 53, 65, 84
Dahomey	9, 28, 36, 58, 64
Denmark	15
Ecuador	22, 62
Egypt	3, 8, 10, 14, 19, 20, 29, 38, 41, 53, 65, 68
Ethiopia	20, 38, 39
Fernando Po	9, 58, 64
France	29, 43, 53
French Somaliland	20, 38, 39
Gabon	9, 28, 36, 42, 58, 64
Gambia	9, 28, 36, 58, 64
Germany	15, 25
Ghana	9, 28, 36, 42, 58, 64
Gibraltar	24, 29, 53, 65
Greece	5, 29, 53, 65, 68
Guatemala	39
Guinea	9, 28, 58, 64
Guyana	12, 71
Holland	43, 52

Country	Key Number
Hong Kong	10
India	3, 14, 19, 20, 38, 45, 63, 72, 74
Indonesia	10, 56, 61
Iran	4, 46, 76
Iraq	4, 46, 76
Israel	29, 53, 65, 84
Italy	5, 29, 35
Ivory Coast	28, 36, 42, 58, 64
Japan	10, 58
Jordan	20
Kenya	20, 38, 39
Korea	10
Kuwait	4, 46, 76
Lebanon	29, 53, 65
Liberia	9, 28, 36, 42, 58, 64
Libya	24, 29, 53, 65
Madeira	28, 36, 64
Malaya	10
Malta	5, 24, 29, 53, 65, 84
Mauritius	20, 38, 39
Mexico	29, 39
Morocco	24, 29, 53, 65
Mozambique	20, 21, 38, 39, 70
New Zealand	6, 11, 32, 57, 67, 73
Nigeria	9, 28, 36, 42, 58, 64
Pakistan	3, 14, 19, 20, 38, 54, 63, 72
Panama	39, 62
Paraguay	47
Peru	22, 23, 62
Philippines	10, 51
Poland	66
Portugal	13, 29, 75
Portuguese West Africa	75
Portuguese Guinea	75
Puerto Rico	69
Romania	29, 53, 65
Russia	80, 82
Sabah	10
Sarawak	10
Saudi Arabia	4, 46, 76
Senegal	9, 28, 36, 42, 58, 64
Sicily	29
Sierra Leone	9, 28, 36, 42, 58, 64
Singapore	10
South Africa	11, 20, 38, 39, 70
South West Africa	20, 38, 39, 70
Spain	31, 37, 50, 79
Spanish Guinea	9, 58, 64
St Helena	20
Sudan	8, 20, 38, 39, 41, 77

Country	Key Number
Surinam	12
Syria	29, 53, 65
Tanzania	20, 38, 39
Thailand	10
Togoland	9, 28, 36, 58, 64
Trucial States	4, 46, 76
Tunisia	24, 29, 53, 65
Turkey	29, 53, 65
Uruguay	30, 44, 47
USA – Atlantic	24, 33, 78, 83
– Pacific	11, 27
– Great Lakes	40
– Gulf Ports	49, 78, 83
Venezuela	39
West Indies	12, 13, 34, 39, 62, 71
Yugoslavia	5, 29

Elder Dempster Line Aureol (1951/14,083grt) prepares to sail to West Africa from Princes Landing Stage.

Number 1
Line: Actanz Line
Service: Australia
Owner/Agent: Gracie Beazley & Co.

Number 2
Line: Alianca Line
Service: Brazil
Owner/Agent: Lamport & Holt Line

Number 3
Line: Anchor Line
Service: Aden; Egypt; India; Pakistan
Owner/Agent: Anchor Line

Number 4
Line: Arya National Shipping Line S.A.
Service: Bahrain; Iran; Iraq; Kuwait; Saudi Arabia; Trucial States
Owner/Agent: Lambert Bros

Number 5
Line: Atlant Line
Service: Greece; Italy – Adriatic; Malta; Yugoslavia
Owner/Agent: Sivewright Bacon & Co.

Number 6
Line: Avenue Line
Service: New Zealand
Owner/Agent: Dowie & Marwood Ltd

Number 7
Line: Aznar Line
Service: Canary Isles
Owner/Agent: Yeoward Bros

Number 8
Line: Bibby Line
Service: Burma; Ceylon; Egypt; Sudan
Owner/Agent: Bibby Bros Ltd

Number 9
Line: Black Star Line
Service: Cameroon; Canary Isles; Congo; Dahomey; Fernando Po; Gabon;
Gambia; Ghana; Guinea; Liberia; Nigeria; Senegal; Sierra Leone;
Spanish Guinea, Togoland
Owner/Agent: Bahr Behrend

Anchor Line Caledonia (1948/11,252grt) is assisted by Alexandra Towing Company tugs at Princes Landing Stage. She was sold in 1965 to become an accommodation vessel in Amsterdam and was broken up in Hamburg in 1970.

Staffordshire (1950/8,685grt) docks at Alfred Dock, Birkenhead to load general cargo for India and Pakistan. She was broken up at Hong Kong in 1971.

Number 10
Line: Blue Funnel Line
Service: China; Egypt; Hong Kong; Indonesia; Japan; Korea; Malaya; Philippines; Sabah; Sarawak; Singapore; Thailand
Owner/Agent: Blue Funnel Line

Number 11
Line: Blue Star Line
Service: (A) New Zealand
(B) Canada; USA; Pacific; South Africa
Owner/Agent: (A) Dowie & Marwood Ltd
(B) Lamport & Holt Line

Number 12
Line: Booker Line
Service: Guyana; Surinam; West Indies – Leeward Isles, Virgin Islands.
Owner/Agent: Booker Line

Number 13
Line: Booth Line
Service: Brazil – North & Amazon Ports; Portugal; West Indies; Barbados; Trinidad.
Owner/Agent: The Booth Steamship Co. Ltd

Number 14
Line: Brocklebank Line
Service: Aden; Egypt; India; Pakistan
Owner/Agent: Cunard-Brocklebank Ltd

Number 15
Line: Bugsier Reederei-Und-Bergungs Akt.
Service: Denmark; Germany
Owner/Agent: Henry Tyrer & Co. Ltd

Number 16
Line: C.P. Ships
Service: Canada – Atlantic Ports, Great Lakes
Owner/Agent: C.P. Ships

Number 17
Line: China National Corporation
Service: China
Owner/Agent: Lambert Bros (Shipping) Ltd

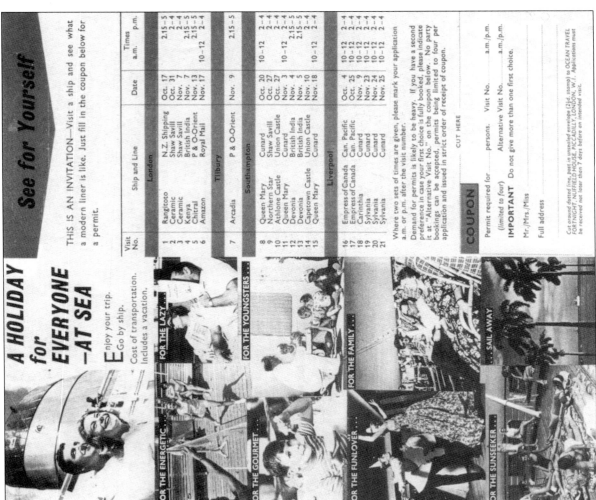

Ocean Travel Fortnight 'visit a ship' programme in 1964.

BIBBY LINE

S.S. "WARWICKSHIRE"
BIRKENHEAD

TO

PORT SAID, PORT SUDAN, COLOMBO
AND

RANGOON

BERTH No. 222 WEST FLOAT, BIRKENHEAD

Telephone: CLAUGHTON 2022

Commence Receiving:
23rd JANUARY, 1961

Closing:
4th FEBRUARY, 1961

Application for space should be made and completed Shipping Note lodged as early as possible with any of the undernoted Offices. Cargo is carried subject to all terms, conditions and exceptions of Shipping Notes, Wharfingers' Receipts and Bills of Lading.

Liverpool: BIBBY BROTHERS & CO.,
Martins Bank Building Water Street.
Telephone: CENtral 0492.

London: ALEXR. HOWDEN & CO. LTD.,
107/112 Leadenhall Street; E.C.3.
Telephone: AVEnue 3444

LONDON to RANGOON
via Birkenhead

m.v. "WORCESTERSHIRE"

Closing : Sheds 11/12, TILBURY DOCK, 11th FEBRUARY, 1961
18th January 1961

Bibby Line Warwickshire sailing list for a voyage to Port Said, Port Sudan, Colombo and Rangoon in 1961.
Opposite: breakfast menu for M.V. Derbyshire on 14 January 1954.

Antenor, Blue Funnel Line 1957
7,974grt, 150m x 19m, 16½kt
She was renamed Glenochy in 1970, Dymas in 1972 and Kaiyun in 1973. Broken up in China in 1983.

BIBBY LINE

BREAKFAST

Papaya
Stewed Apricots   Stewed Figs

Quaker Oats   Cornflakes
Puffed Wheat   Shredded Wheat

Fillet Haddock en Creme

American Hash Cake
Grilled Bacon
- TO ORDER -
Eggs:- Fried, Turned, Buttered Poached
Omelettes:- Plain, Parsley, Tomato

Griddle Cakes
White & Graham Rolls
Toast   Marmalade   Honey
Tea   Cocoa   Coffee
****

m.v. "DERBYSHIRE"   14th January, 1954

Southland Star, Blue Star Line 1967
11,300grt, 168m x 22m, 21kt
168m x 22m Broken up at Chittagong in 1993.

Number 18
Line
Service
Owner/Agent

China Ocean Shipping Co.
China
Lambert Bros (Shipping) Ltd

Number 19
Line
Service
Owner/Agent

City Line
Aden; Egypt; India; Pakistan
Hall Line

Number 20
Line
Service

Owner/Agent

Clan Line
Aden; Angola; Ascension Island; Canary Isles; Ceylon; Egypt;
Ethiopia; French Somaliland; India; Jordan; Kenya; Mauritius;
Mozambique; Pakistan; South Africa; St Helena; Sudan; Tanzania
Cayzer Irvine & Co. Ltd

Number 21
Line
Service
Owner/Agent

Companhia Nacional De Navegacao
Mozambique
Leopold Walford Ltd

Number 22
Line
Service
Owner/Agent

Companhia Peruana de Vapores
Chile; Colombia; Ecuador; Peru
Benj. Ackerley & Son Ltd,

Number 23
Line
Service
Owner/Agent

Companhia Sud-Americana de Vapores
Chile; Peru
Vogt. & Maguire Ltd

Number 24
Line
Service

Owner/Agent

Cunard Line
USA – Atlantic Ports; Gibraltar; Libya; Malta; Morocco; Tunisia;
Algeria
Cunard-Brocklebank Ltd

Number 25
Line
Service
Owner/Agent

Currie Line
Germany
Henry Tyrer & Co. Ltd

for the HOLIDAY of a Lifetime

1972 Cruises Programme

(PROVISIONAL ITINERARIES)

You can't help but enjoy the marvellous, informal atmosphere of the Monte Umbe; meeting people of your own age and interests, pleasing yourself and letting others do the work.

The 14,000 ton Monte Umbe carries 300 passengers in single, double, three or four berth cabins, all beautifully finished and air conditioned.

ENTERTAINMENT BY DAY AND NIGHT

By day there are deck games, two swimming pools or sunbathing to occupy your time. Or you can escape the heat and relax in one of the duty free bars or luxury lounges.

By night you can dance either in the night club, or to the resident trio; or share a long, cool drink in the bars.

FOOD OF A LIFETIME

We take special pride in the quality and variety of our meals — both English and Continental. You can start the day with English breakfast — relax through a four course lunch — and crown every memorable day with a five course dinner of banquet quality — AND bottles of red and white wine are served FREE at every meal.

TO CARE FOR YOU

The Monte Umbe carries a doctor and two nurses plus hostesses, full laundry facilities and ladies' and gentlemen's hairdressing salons

CANARY CRUISE 1 June—15 June	ATLANTIC CRUISE 16 June—29 June	MADEIRA CRUISE 30 June—14 July	SPECIAL MEDITERRANEAN CRUISE 14 July—1 August	MALAGA CRUISE 2 Aug.—17 Aug.	FIESTA CRUISE 18 Aug.—2 Sept.	AFRICAN CRUISE 4 Sept.—18 Sept	CORUNNA CRUISE 19 Sept.—3 Oct	TANGIER CRUISE 4 Oct.—19 Oct.
Liverpool	Liverpool	Liverpool	Liverpool	Liverpool	Liverpool	Liverpool	Liverpool	Liverpool
Cadiz	Vigo	Dublin	Cadiz	Dublin	Dublin	Dublin	Dublin	Cadiz
Tenerife	Tenerife	Arrecife	Naples	Cadiz	Vigo	Lisbon	Corunna	Tangier
Las Palmas	Las Palmas	Las Palmas	Malaga	Malaga	Madeira	Casablanca	Madeira	Las Palmas
Arrecife	Arrecife	Tenerife	Vigo	Las Palmas	Tenerife	Las Palmas	Tenerife	Tenerife
Corunna	Corunna	Madeira	Liverpool	Tenerife	Las Palmas	Tenerife	Las Palmas	Vigo
Liverpool	Liverpool	Liverpool		Liverpool	Corunna	Liverpool	Vigo	Liverpool
					Dublin		Liverpool	
					Liverpool			

Prices are exactly the same as for the Autumn Cruises 1971, with the sole exception of the Special Mediterranean Cruise for which, because of its duration—17 day —a supplement of £10 will be charged on these 197 fares.

1972 Aznar Line cruise programme from Liverpool and Dublin.

Diversification by Harland and Wolff, Bootle in 1970.

70

Clan Macgregor (1962/9,039grt) and Clan MacLennan (1947/6,366grt) berthed together at the Clan Line berth in Vittoria Dock, Birkenhead. In 1981 Clan MacGregor was the last Clan liner in service. She became Angelika R in 1982 and was broken up in Greece in 1983. Clan MacLennan was broken up at Shanghai in 1971.

Empress of England Canadian Pacific Steamships 1957
25,585grt, 195m x 26m, 21kt
She became Ocean Monarch in 1970 and was broken up in 1975.

Number 26
Line: Dolphin Line
Service: Australia
Owner/Agent: Dowie & Marwood Ltd

Number 27
Line: East Asiatic Co. Ltd
Service: Canada and USA – Pacific Ports
Owner/Agent: Escombe McGrath & Co. Ltd

Number 28
Line: Elder Dempster Lines
Service: Angola; Cameroon; Canary Isles; Congo; Dahomey; Gabon; Gambia; Ghana; Guinea; Ivory Coast; Liberia; Madeira; Nigeria; Senegal; Sierra Leone; Togoland
Owner/Agent: Elder Dempster Lines

Number 29
Line: Ellerman Line
Service: Albania; Algeria; Bulgaria; Cyprus; Egypt; Gibralter; Greece; Israel; Italy; Lebanon; Libya; Malta; Morocco; Portugal; Romania; Sicily; Syria; Tunisia; Turkey; Yugoslavia
Owner/Agent: Ellerman & Papayanni Lines

Number 30
Line: E.L.M.A.
Service: Argentina; Uruguay
Owner/Agent: Lamport & Holt Line

Number 31
Line: Euromar Line
Service: Spain
Owner/Agent: S. William Coe & Co. Ltd

Number 32
Line: Federal Line
Service: New Zealand
Owner/Agent: Dowie & Marwood Ltd

Number 33
Line: Furness Warren Line
Service: Canada – Newfoundland, Nova Scotia; USA
Owner/Agent: Furness Withy & Co. Ltd

Canadian Pacific Steamships official notice advertising loading details for the maiden voyage of the new Empress of Canada.

Canadian Pacific

MAIDEN VOYAGE

EMPRESS OF CANADA

LIVERPOOL · QUEBEC & MONTREAL · MONDAY, APRIL 24, 1961

Receiving Cargo April 15 - April 20.

Loading Berth—North No. 1 Gladstone Dock, Liverpool.

SUPERB PASSENGER ACCOMMODATION—FULLY AIR-CONDITIONED—FIRST CLASS AND TOURIST. SHIPPERS' ENQUIRIES DIRECT OR THROUGH THEIR USUAL AGENTS, WILL RECEIVE IMMEDIATE ATTENTION

FAST SERVICE: This vessel is scheduled to maintain a six days' passage between Liverpool and Montreal.

THROUGH BILLS OF LADING: Through Bills of Lading are issued to inland destinations in Canada and U.S.A.

CANADIAN PACIFIC EXPRESS: Merchandise, samples, livestock and valuables sent by Express Service to all parts of Canada and U.S.A.

Goods are received for shipment only subject to the terms and conditions of the Company's usual form of Wharfinger's receipt and/or Bill of Lading.

For rates and information apply:—

CANADIAN PACIFIC RAILWAY CO.

Royal Liver Building, Liverpool, or any other Canadian Pacific Office, a list of which is overleaf.

Subject to change without notice

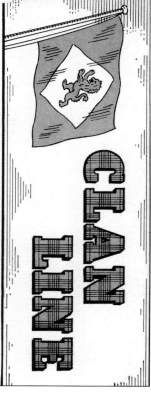

CLAN LINE

T.S.S. CLAN CUMMING

WILL CLOSE FOR CARGO AT

GLASGOW   BIRKENHEAD

Jan. 10th   Jan. 18th

FOR

AQABA • ADEN
BOMBAY
COCHIN • COLOMBO

Intending Shippers wishing to ship Cargo by this vessel should make application for space on the appropriate form which can be obtained and lodged at any of the undermentioned Offices. Shippers must not despatch Cargo to vessels until receipt of calling forward notice. It is essential that Shippers and Suppliers should adhere to the delivery dates shown on such notices.

Vessel has liberty to call at other U.K. Ports and at other Ports either on or out of route.

All Cargo carried by Special Agreement only and subject to all terms, conditions and exceptions of shipping notes, wharfingers' receipts and Bills of Lading.

Cool Chamber and Refrigerator Cargo can be accepted by arrangement.

Goods insured on the most favourable Terms.

Special accommodation for Livestock

Freight payable in exchange for Bills of Lading.

CAYZER, IRVINE & CO., LTD.

2 ST. MARY AXE
ROYAL LIVER BUILDING
109 HOPE STREET

BRITISH & COMMONWEALTH (AGENCIES) LTD.

		Tel: AVE 2010
	LONDON, E.C.3	CEN 5861
	LIVERPOOL	CEN 7050
	GLASGOW, C.2.	
Do.	MANCHESTER	Deansgate 7891
Do.	BIRMINGHAM	Midland 8271
Do.	SHEFFIELD	Sheffield 25880
	LEEDS	Leeds 25790
JONES, HEARD & CO., LTD.	NEWPORT, MON.	Newport 64011
SIMPSON BROS. (SWANSEA) LTD.	SWANSEA	Swansea 50321
WM. BROWN, ATKINSON & CO. LTD.	HULL	CEN 36921

GLASGOW, 20th December, 1960.

Clan Line sailing list advertising T.S.S Clan Cumming sailing to Aqaba, Aden, Bombay, Cochin and Colombo in January 1961.

Cunard Line conventional cargo vessels Samaria (1965/5,837grt), Parthia (1963/5,586grt) and Media (1963/5,586grt) load cargo at the company berth in Huskisson Dock.

Kumba, Elder Dempster Line 1958
5,439grt, 139m x 18m, 12½kt
She became Regent Liberty in 1974 and arrived at Visakhapatnam in India for scrapping on 24 January 1980.

Number 34
Line   Geest Line
Service   West Indies – Windward Isles
Owner/Agent   Geest Line

Number 35
Line   Glynn Line
Service   Italy
Owner/Agent   John Glynn & Son Ltd

Number 36
Line   Guinea Gulf Line
Service   Angola; Cameroon; Canary Isles; Congo; Dahomey; Gabon; Gambia; Ghana; Ivory Coast; Liberia; Madeira; Nigeria; Senegal; Sierra Leone; Togo
Owner/Agent   Elder Dempster Lines Ltd'

Number 37
Line   Golfo Line
Service   Spain – Northern
Owner/Agent   Houlder Bros & Co. Ltd

Number 38
Line   Hall Line
Service   Aden; Angola; Canary Isles; Egypt; Ethiopia; French Somaliland; India; Kenya; Mauritius; Mozambique; Pakistan; South Africa; South West Africa; Sudan; Tanzania
Owner/Agent   Hall Line

Number 39
Line   Harrison Line
Service   Aden; Angola; British Honduras; Colombia; Ethiopia; French Somaliland; Guatemala; Kenya; Mauritius; Mexico; Mozambique; Panama; South Africa; South West Africa; Sudan; Tanzania; Venezuela; West Indies – Barbados; Curacao; Trinidad
Owner/Agent   Thos. & Jas. Harrison Ltd

Number 40
Line   Head Line
Service   USA – Great Lakes
         Canada – Great Lakes
Owner/Agent   G. Heyn & Sons (GB) Ltd

If you're looking for

Leisure, Pleasure, Sun, Fun

sunscape to West Africa on Elder Dempster's passenger liner *Aureol*.

This winter you have a choice. You can stay at home and enjoy the smog, the fog, the snow and ice, the freezing nights of a dreary British Winter — if that's your idea of enjoyment. Elder Dempster has a

better idea **Leisure, Pleasure, Sun, Fun**

escape by *Aureol* to Nigeria. The sun drenched 'Land of the Mighty River'. At sea you'll find hot sun, blue skies, and a soft summer breeze. Just relax. Fill your lungs with sparkling fresh air and soak up the generous sun . . . and think of the others back home.

Elder Dempster Line brochure for passenger services from Liverpool to West Africa in 1962.

77

CUNARD LINE

Principal Offices and Agencies

GREAT BRITAIN AND IRELAND

			Tel. Address and Telephone Nos.
LIVERPOOL, 3	...	Cunard Bldg., Pier Head ...	Cunardliner, Maritime 3000
LONDON, S.W.1	...	Cunard Bldg., 15 Lower Regent Street (Nr. Piccadilly Circus)	Cunarlon, Picey Whitehall 7890
LONDON, E.C.3	...	Cunard House, 88 Leadenhall Street	Cunardstar, Fen Avenue 3010
BIRMINGHAM, 2	...	8 Temple Street	Cunardstar, Midland 2881
BRADFORD, 1	...	Britannia House, Broadway	Cunardstar Bradford 27134
BRISTOL, 1	...	Mauretania Bldg., 11 Park Street	Cunardstar Bristol 29031/3
COBH	...	West Beach	Cunardstar, Cork 81125/6/7
DUBLIN	...	40 Dawson Street	Cunardstar, Dublin 76481'5
GLASGOW, C1	...	25 St. Vincent Place	Cunardstar, Central 3983
MANCHESTER, 3	...	75 Deansgate	Cunardstar, Deansgate 8731
PLYMOUTH	...	Royal London House, 153 & 155 Armada Way	Cunardstar Plymouth 64770
SOUTHAMPTON	...	Maritime Chambers, Canute Road	Cunardstar Southampton 21351
SELFAST, 1	...	Little, Whiting & Tedford Ltd., 74 High Street	Cunardstar Belfast 24455/6

EUROPE

AMSTERDAM	...	Hoyman & Schuurman, Rokin, 90
BARCELONA, 11	...	Viajes Marsans S.A., Rambla 134/136
BRUSSELS	...	Cie. Deru-Ocean Travel Bureau, 24 Rue de Namur
CHERBOURG	...	The Cunard Steam-Ship Co. Ltd., Cunard White Star, 32 Quai Alexandre III
COPENHAGEN	...	The Cunard Steam-Ship Co. Ltd., Vimmelskaftet, 42C (Lerck's Passage)
FRANKFURT	...	The Cunard Steam-Ship Co. Ltd., Industrie House, Taunusstrasse, 52
HAMBURG	...	The Cunard Steam-Ship Co. Ltd. Jungfernstieg 7
HAVRE	...	The Cunard White Star, 49 Rue Lord Kitchener
HELSINKI	...	Finland Steam-Ship Co. Ltd.
LISBON	...	Sociedade Comercial Garland Laidley S.A.R.L. 10 Travessa do Corpo Santo
LUCERNE, 2	...	Cunard Line, A. G. Schwanenplatz 8
LUXEMBOURG	...	Bureau de Voyage, Emile Wenkel, 57 Boulevard Royal
MADRID	...	Viajes Marsans S.A., Carrera San Jeronimo, 34
OSLO	...	The Cunard Steam-Ship Co. Ltd., Toldbugaten 2 (Oslo Bors.)
PARIS	...	The Cunard Steam-Ship Co. Ltd., Cunard White Star, 6 Rue Scribe
ROME	...	Cunard S.p.A., 83-85 Via Barberini
ROTTERDAM	...	Rays & Co., Veerhaven 4
STOCKHOLM	...	Nyman & Schultz Travel Bureau, Arsenalsgatan 4
VIENNA	...	The Cunard Steam-Ship Co. Ltd., Karntnering 4

Consult your travel agent

PRINTED IN ENGLAND 82259

CROSS CHANNEL TRIP by CUNARD

WORLD'S LARGEST LINER

Including the "QUEENS"

Cherbourg — Cobh — Liverpool — Havre — Southampton — Rotterdam

Cross Channel trips by Cunard Line vessels from Cobh, Liverpool and Southampton in 1965.

Houlder Brothers and Ellerman & Papayanni Lines vessels in Alexandra Dock, Liverpool during the national seamens strike in 1966.

Essex, Federal Steamship Company 1954
10,936grt, 160m x 21m, 16kt
She was renamed Golden Gulf in 1975 and broken up at Gadani Beach in 1977.

Number 41
Line   Henderson Line
Service   Aden; Burma; Egypt; Sudan
Owner/Agent Bibby Bros & Co.

Number 42
Line   Hoegh Line
Service   Cameroon; Gabon; Ghana; Ivory Coast; Liberia; Nigeria; Senegal; Sierra Leone
Owner/Agent Brown Jenkinson & Co

Number 43
Line   Holland Steamship Company
Service   Belgium; Holland; France
Owner/Agent Lamport & Holt Line Ltd

Number 44
Line   Houlder Line
Service   Argentina; Uruguay
Owner/Agent Houlder Bros. & Co. Ltd

Number 45
Line   India Steamship Co. Ltd
Service   India
Owner/Agent Henry Tyrer & Co. Ltd

Number 46
Line   Kuwait Shipping Co.
Service   Bahrain; Iran; Iraq; Kuwait; Saudi Arabia; Trucial States
Owner/Agent Benjamin Ackerley & Son Ltd

Number 47
Line   Lamport & Holt Line
Service   Argentina; Brazil; Paraguay; Uruguay
Owner/Agent Lamport & Holt Line Ltd

Number 48
Line   Lloyd Brasiliero
Service   Brazil
Owner/Agent Kersten Hunik & Co. Ltd

FURNESS Warren Line

SERVES

CANADA U·S·A

AGENCY:—

ONE WAY FARES

Summer Season Rates in RED
Off Season Rates in BLACK

To ST. JOHN'S N.F., HALIFAX, N.S., and BOSTON, Mass.

Effective for sailings on and after 1st April, 1958.
Up to and including 31st October, 1958, westbound; and 31st August, 1958, eastbound.

R.M.S. "NOVA SCOTIA"
AND
R.M.S. "NEWFOUNDLAND"

(Subject to alteration without notice)

FIRST CLASS

	1 ADULT	2 ADULTS	3 ADULTS	BERTH RATE
"A" Deck				
Suite A2, with sitting room and bath	£164	£234	£270	£90
	£178	£256	£300	£100
Single Rooms, A1, A3, A4, A5, A6, A7, A8, A9 with shower & toilet	£87	—	—	£87
	£97			£97
Double Rooms A10, A11, A12, A15, with shower & toilet	£110	£158	—	£79
	£121	£176		£88
"B" Deck				
Single Room B18	£81	—	—	£81
	£90			£90
Double Rooms B20, B24, B25, B28, B29 with shower and toilet	£110	£158	—	£79
	£121	£176		£88
Double Room B33	£97	£144	—	£72
	£107	£162		£81
Three Berth, Rooms B31, B35, with shower & toilet	£110	£158	£228	£76
	£121	£176	£255	£85
Three Berth Rooms B14, B16, B17, B22, B31, B26, B27, B31	£97	£144	£208/10	£69/10
	£107	£162	£235/10	£78/10

TOURIST CLASS from £53/10 Off Season
£59 Summer Season

SUMMER SEASON PERIODS 1958
WESTBOUND — 1st JUNE to 31st OCTOBER incl.
EASTBOUND — 1st APRIL to 31st AUGUST incl.

CHILDREN'S FARES—BOTH CLASSES

			1 year and under 12 years—Half Fare
Under 1 year	£3 0 0		12 years and over—Full Fare
First Class	£3 10 0		
Tourist Class			

RATES FOR DOGS, CATS, CYCLES ETC.

Dogs (large or small) each £8 0 0
Cats (in baskets) each £3 10 0
Birds (one or two in cage) £3 10 0
Bicycles (one or two in cage) £3 10 0
Perambulators £3 10 0
Bicycles £1 18 0

Powered vehicles up to 100
Powered vehicles from 100
Powered vehicles from 200 up to 400 lb.

Other rates on application

Furness Warren Line brochure for passenger services by Nova Scotia and Newfoundland to Canada and USA.

PASSENGER SERVICES

- Monthly sailings from Liverpool and London for Brazil and River Plate.

- Passenger opportunities on regular sailings between Argentina, Uruguay, Brazil, Amazon Ports and New York.

- Round Voyages of three to four months arranged enabling you to see South America and at the same time conserve currency by using the ship as an hotel.

- Experienced staff to advise on regulations in force at home and abroad regarding currency, customs and passport formalities etc.

- Itineraries planned and arrangements made for reservations on connecting steamers and airlines.

For full particulars of sailings and fares apply to:—

LAMPORT & HOLT LINE LTD.

Head Office :
Royal Liver Building, LIVERPOOL, 3.
CENtral 5650

and at

85 Gracechurch Street, LONDON E.C.3
MANsion House 7533

64 Cross Street, MANCHESTER
BLAckfriars 7674

Britannia House, Leeds Road, BRADFORD
Bradford 22527

Lamport & Holt Line brochure for passenger sailings from Liverpool and London to Brazil, Uruguay and Argentina.

City Of Pretoria, Hall Line 1947
8,450grt, 152m x 20m, 16kt
Sold in 1967 and renamed *Proxenion* and broken up later that year in Japan.

Wanderer, Harrison Line 1951
8,150grt, 140m x 18m, 12kt
Renamed *Cleopatra* in 1970 and *Chung Thai* in 1974. Broken up in South Korea in 1974

Number 49
Line   Lykes Line
Service   USA – Gulf Ports
Owner/Agent Dowie & Marwood Ltd

Number 50
Line   MacAndrews Line
Service   Spain
Owner/Agent MacAndrews & Co. Ltd

Number 51
Line   Maritime Company Of The Philippines
Service   Philippines
Owner/Agent Mann & Son (London) Ltd

Number 52
Line   Metric Line
Service   Belgium; Holland
Owner/Agent Lamport & Holt Line Ltd

Number 53
Line   Moss Hutchison Line
Service   Algeria; Bulgaria; Cyprus; Egypt; France; Gibraltar; Greece; Israel; Lebanon; Libya; Malta; Morocco; Romania; Syria; Tunisia; Turkey
Owner/Agent Moss Hutchison Line Ltd

Number 54
Line   National Shipping Corporation Karachi (Pakistan)
Service   Pakistan
Owner/Agent Escombe McGrath & Co. Ltd

Number 55
Line   Navigation Maritime Bulgare
Service   Bulgaria
Owner/Agent Cory Bros & Co. Ltd

Number 56.
Line   Nederlandsche Stoomvaart Maatschappij Oceaan N.V.
Service   Indonesia
Owner/Agent Ocean Steamship Co. Ltd

HALL and CITY LINES

KARACHI AND BOMBAY

KARACHI & BOMBAY

Hall and City Line sailing lists for sailings from the North Quay, West Float, Birkenhead.

HENDERSON LINE

PORT SAID

SUEZ

PORT SUDAN

ADEN AND RANGOON

S.S. "YOMA"

	Commence Receiving	Closes for Cargo
Glasgow, (No. 6 PRINCE'S DOCK)	28th Feb.	7th Mar.
Birkenhead, (WEST FLOAT)	6th Mar.	14th Mar.

Refrigerator space available.

Application forms for space should be lodged as soon as possible with any of the undernoted Offices. Cargo is received and carried subject to all the terms, conditions and liabilities contained in our standard forms of Shipping notes, Wharfinger's Receipt and Bill of Lading to which the attention of Shippers is particularly drawn.

P. HENDERSON & CO.,
Glasgow,
95 Bothwell Street, C.2.
Telephone CENTRAL 870

London,
4 Fenchurch Avenue, E.C.3.
Telephone MANSION HOUSE 4166

Liverpool,
Wellington Buildings, The Strand, 2.
Telephone MARITIME 5481

Birmingham, J. Johnson & Co. Ltd., 82/3 Suffolk Street.
Manchester, Thos. & Jno. Brocklebank Ltd., 57 Princess Street.
Bradford, Lamport & Holt Line Ltd., Howard House, Bank Street.
Sheffield, R. Thomas & Co. (Bradford) Ltd., Room 12, Cambridge Chambers, Cambridge Street, 1.
Swansea, T. H. Couch Ltd., 6 & 6a Wind Street.
Newport, (Mon.) Jones, Heard & Co. Ltd., 107 Dock Street.
Dundee, Thos. & Jno. Brocklebank Ltd., 8 Panmure Street.

	Telephone
	Midland 3671
	Central 3789
	18868
	23333
	5W31
	64911
	28801

Next Henderson Line Sailings:—

		Closing
s.s. "MARTABAN"	27th Mar.	GLASGOW 30th Mar.
	11th Apr.	BIRKENHEAD
s.s. "SALWEEN"	—	SWANSEA 1st May
	—	9th May

20th February, 1961

HOULDER LINE

RIVER PLATE

FAST DIRECT SERVICE

(NOT CALLING AT BRAZILIAN PORTS)

LIVERPOOL

Via
BRISTOL CHANNEL
LAS PALMAS
(If sufficient inducement)

TO MONTEVIDEO & BUENOS AIRES

TAKING CARGO BY TRANSHIPMENT TO ROSARIO, UP RIVER, AND PATAGONIAN PORTS

M.V. "THORPE GRANGE"

Dates for Heavy Lifts on application

Commencing to receive cargo	-	Wed. 28th December, 1960
Closing for cargo	-	Wed. 4th January, 1961
Sailing	-	Sat. 7th January, 1961

LOADING BERTH—SOUTH-WEST, No. 3, ALEXANDRA DOCK

To be followed by M.V. "SHAFTESBURY" sailing 19th January, 1961

For Freight, Passage and Insurance apply to

HOULDER BROTHERS & CO., LTD.

Head Office :—53, Leadenhall Street, London, E.C.3.

Branch Offices :

LIVERPOOL	Royal Liver Building
BELFAST	Aires, McHenison & Co., Waring Street
	26/31, Waring Street
BIRMINGHAM	Waterloo House, Waterloo St.
HULL	69 Market Street
MANCHESTER	44, King Street
SHEFFIELD	Norfolk Row
	Prudential Buildings,
SWANSEA	Castle Street
GLASGOW	19 St. Vincent Place

Telex : 28526 & 28361
Telegrams : "HOULDERS," TELEX, LONDON."
"HOULDERS"

Telephones :
Royal 2020 (40 lines)
Trunks 176

Tel. Add.: HOULDERS
Telephone CENTRAL 7151

LIVERPOOL, ROYAL LIVER BUILDING

Representaciones in Argentina and Uruguay : Soc. Anon., Houlder Brothers & Co. (Argentina), Ltd.,
Buenos Aires, Rosario de Santa Fe, La Plata, Montevideo

And at Cape Town, Sydney (N.S.W.)

21/12/60

Ocean Transport, Houlder Brothers 1962
8,608grt, 141m x 19m, 15kt
Renamed Ellion Hop in 1979 and broken
up in 1983.

Rubens, Lamport & Holt Line 1951
4,472grt, 125m x 17m, 12½kt
Built as Crispin and renamed Mandowi in 1953. She was renamed Dunstan and Rubens in 1966
and Irini K in 1973. Broken up in Istanbul in 1974.

Number 57
Line: New Zealand Shipping Co. Ltd
Service: New Zealand
Owner/Agent: Dowie & Marwood Ltd

Number 58
Line: Nigerian National Shipping Line
Service: Cameroon; Dahomey; Fernando Po; Gabon; Gambia; Ghana; Guinea; Ivory Coast; Liberia; Nigeria; Senegal; Sierra Leone; Spanish Guinea; Togoland
Owner/Agent: Nigerian National Shipping Line Ltd

Number 59
Line: Nippon Yusen Kaisha Line
Service: Japan
Owner/Agent: Gellatly, Hankey & Co. Ltd

Number 60
Line: Ocean Wide Shipping Co. Ltd
Service: Canada – Great Lakes; Atlantic Coast Ports
Owner/Agent: Gellatly, Hankey & Co. Ltd

Number 61
Line: P.N. Djakarta Lloyd Line
Service: Indonesia
Owner/Agent: Henry Tyrer & Co. Ltd

Number 62
Line: Pacific Steam Navigation Co.
Service: Bermuda; Chile; Colombia; Equador; Panama; Peru; West Indies; Bahamas
Owner/Agent: Furness Withy & Co. Ltd

Number 63
Line: Pakistan Shipping Line
Service: India; Pakistan
Owner/Agent: Brown Jenkinson & Co.

Number 64
Line: Palm Line
Service: Angola; Cameroon; Canary Isles; Congo; Dahomey; Fernando Po; Gabon; Gambia; Ghana; Guinea; Ivory Coast; Liberia; Madeira; Senegal; Nigeria; Sierra Leone; Spanish Guinea; Togoland
Owner/Agent: Palm Line Ltd

Memphis, Moss Hutchinson Line 1947
3,575grt, 111m x 16m, 13½kt
Renamed Elias in 1972 and was broken up in Karachi in 1981, where demolition began at Gadani Beach on 7 December 1981.

Honorata, New Zealand Shipping 1942
12,090grt, 168m x 21m, 16kt
On 13 December 1942 she was torpedoed by U103 off the Azores. She later sailed to Liverpool where she was repaired. Sold in 1967, renamed Nor and was scrapped at Kaohsiung.

Number 65
Line: Papayanni Line
Service: Algeria; Bulgaria; Cyprus; Egypt; Gibraltar; Greece; Israel; Lebanon; Libya; Malta; Morocco; Romania; Syria; Tunisia; Turkey
Owner/Agent: Ellerman & Papayanni Line Ltd

Number 66
Line: Polish Steamship Company Ltd
Service: Poland
Owner/Agent: W.H. Stott & Co. Ltd

Number 67
Line: Port Line
Service: New Zealand
Owner/Agent: Gracie Beazley & Co. Ltd

Number 68
Line: Red Rose Line
Service: Egypt; Greece
Owner/Agent: Khedivial Mail Line (Agency) Ltd

Number 69
Line: Royal Mail Line
Service: Puerto Rico
Owner/Agent: Furness Withy & Co. Ltd

Number 70
Line: Safmarine Line
Service: Mozambique; South Africa; South West Africa
Owner/Agent: A. Coker & Co. Ltd

Number 71
Line: Saguenay Shipping Ltd
Service: Guyana; West Indies; Barbados; Trinidad
Owner/Agent: Bahr Behrend & Co. Ltd

Number 72
Line: Scindia Steam Navigation Co. Ltd
Service: India; Pakistan
Owner/Agent: Bahr Bahrend & Co. Ltd

Number 73
Line: Shaw Savill Line
Service: New Zealand
Owner/Agent: Gracie Beazley & Co. Ltd

Pizarro, Pacific Steam Navigation 1955
8,564grt, 156m x 20m, 18kt
Renamed Kavo Pieratis in 1972 and broken up at Kaohsiung in 1974.

Port Huon Port Line 1965
8,362grt, 149m x 21m, 18kt
Became Julietta in 1972 and Amana in 1984. She was renamed Mana in 1994 and broken up at Alang where she was beached on 10 February.

Number 74
Line   Shipping Corporation Of India Ltd
Service   India
Owner/Agent Henry Tyrer & Co. Ltd

Number 75
Line   Sociedade Geral
Service   Portugal; Portuguese West Africa; Portuguese Guinea; Cape Verde Isles
Owner/Agent E.H. Mundy & Co. Ltd

Number 76
Line   Strick & Ellerman Line
Service   Bahrain; Iran; Iraq; Kuwait; Saudi Arabia; Trucial States
Owner/Agent F.C. Strick & Co.

Number 77
Line   Sudan Shipping Line Ltd
Service   Sudan
Owner/Agent Gellatly Hankey & Co. Ltd

Number 78
Line   Swedish Atlantic Line
Service   USA – Atlantic – Gulf Ports
Owner/Agent Escombe McGrath & Co. Ltd

Number 79
Line   Trafrume Line
Service   Spain
Owner/Agent Leinster & Co. (Liverpool) Ltd

Number 80
Line   U.S.S.R. Lines
Service   Russia – Baltic
Owner/Agent Bahr Behrend & Co. Ltd

Number 81
Line   Union of Burma Five Star Line Corporation Ltd
Service   Burma
Owner/Agent Brown Jenkinson & Co. Ltd

Number 82
Line   Union Baltic Corporation
Service   Russia – Baltic
Owner/Agent Bahr Behrend & Co. Ltd

S.A. Van Der Stel *Safmarine 1966*
10,524grt, 165m x 23m, 20kt
Broken up at Kaohsiung where she arrived on 27 September 1984.

Carnatic *Shaw Savill Line 1956*
11,144grt, 156m x 21m, 17kt
In 1973 she became Darro and Litska K in 1977. Renamed Dimitra in 1979 and was broken up that year.

Number 83	
Line	Wilhelm Wilhelmsen Line
Service	USA – Atlantic – Gulf Ports
Owner/Agent	Escombe McGrath & Co. Ltd
Number 84	
Line	Zim Lines
Service	Cyprus; Israel; Malta
Owner/Agent	Bahr Behrend & Co. Ltd

Regular Coastwise Services

1971

Line	Belfast Steamship Co. Ltd
Service	Northern Ireland – Belfast
Owner/Agent	Coast Lines Ltd
Line	British & Irish Steam Packet Co. Ltd
Service	Dublin
Owner/Agent	Coast Lines Ltd
Line	Irish & Mersey Line
Service	Southern Ireland – Dublin
Owner/Agent	Irish & Mersey Steamship Co. Ltd
Line	Isle Of Man Steam Packet Co. Ltd
Service	Isle of Man
Owner/Agent	Thomas Orford & Son
Line	Limerick Steamship Co. Ltd
Service	Southern Ireland – Limerick
Owner/Agent	Limerick Steamship Co. Ltd

Armanistan Strick Line 1965
8,531grt, 148m x 19m, 16kt
Built as Elysia she became Armanistan in 1968, Strathavoch in 1975 and Sharp Island in 1978.
Broken up at Kaohsiung in 1983.

City Of Eastbourne Hall Line 1962
9,704grt, 155m x 20m, 17½kt
Renamed City Of Toronto in 1971 and Kota Cantik in 1978. Broken up at Kaohsiung in 1984.

Ulster Monarch Belfast Steamship Company 1929
3,815grt, 109m x 14m, 17kt
Broken up in 1966.

The Isle of Man Steam Packet Co. Ltd.

(Incorporated in the Isle of Man)

Excursions by Sea

to ISLE OF MAN and NORTH WALES

Summer Season 1971

Day Excursions
Party Outings
School Educational Parties

between
LIVERPOOL and DOUGLAS
LIVERPOOL and LLANDUDNO
LLANDUDNO and DOUGLAS
HEYSHAM and DOUGLAS

Relax, and Enjoy the Pleasure of a Sea Cruise

Liverpool and Llandudno

This service operates on Sundays, 30th May and 6th June and every Sunday, 20th June to 12th September inclusive, Tuesdays, 8th June to 24th August inclusive also Tuesday, 7th September and every Thursday, 10th June to 26th August, inclusive.

The steamer leaves Liverpool Landing Stage at 10.45 hours weekdays and 11.15 hours on Sundays and the journey takes about 2½ hours.

On leaving Princes Landing Stage the steamer proceeds towards the Bar Lightship affording an excellent view of the Dock System on both sides of the river Mersey.

On approaching Llandudno which has been aptly termed "The Naples of the North" passengers will be enchanted by a view of the Bay framed on one side by the Great Orme and the Little Orme on the other.

The departure time for the return journey is dependent on the state of the tide at Llandudno and details of any particular sailing can be obtained on application.

FARES

Day Excursion   £1.70   (34/-)
(Children 3 and under 14 years half-fare)
Contract Ticket for Season   £20
Book of 10 Day-trip Vouchers £14

PARTY RATES

For parties between 8 and
50 persons   £1.60   (32/-)
For parties of over 50 persons £1.50 (30/-)

Cruises from Llandudno

The two-hour Cruise last year proved very popular and we are continuing the service this year, indeed we have greatly increased the number of cruises which we are sure you will enjoy.

The steamer leaves Llandudno at 14.30 hours on a TWO-HOUR CRUISE to Puffin Island, Red Wharf Bay and proceeding towards Point Lynas, returning to the Pier at approximately 16.30 hours.

As the vessel backs out from Llandudno we look at the rocky and grassy slopes of the Great Orme and towards its extremity the high cliff walls weathered by the years of fierce battering by the elements is the formation of a profile likeness of the beloved Queen Victoria.

(see over)

Isle of Man excursions by sea brochure for 1971.

MENU

HIGH TEA

9/-   9/-

Fillet of Plaice or Halibut Steak

Crinkle Cut Potatoes

COLD:

Pressed Ox Tongue   Boiled Ham   Roast Beef

Roast Lamb   Roast Pork

Salad in Season

or

Crinkle Cut Potatoes

Fruit Salad with Ice Cream

or

Biscuits and Cheese

White and Brown Bread   Toast   Butter

Preserves   Tea   Coffee

Specials to Order:

2/6 Extra   Grilled Steak   2 Lamb Chops

3/- Extra   Mixed Grill

High tea menu for the Isle of Man car ferry Ben My Chree maiden voyage on 12 May 1966.

Munster British & Irish Steam Packet 1968
4,230grt, 110m x 18m, 21kt
Sold in 1983 and renamed Farah and Farah 1. Sold to Chineses interests in 1991 and became Tian Peng.

Isle of Man Steam Packet passenger vessels Ben My Chree (1927/2,586grt) and Lady Of Mann (1930/3,104grt) berthed at the north end of Princes Landing Stage.

Coastal Guardian Environment Agency 1992
47grt, 16m x 6m, 10kt

Cervantes Reederei Heinz KG. 1994
5,026grt, 117m x 18m, 16½kt

THE LIVERPOOL & NORTH WALES STEAMSHIP COMPANY LTD.

Telegrams: "ST. TUDNO, LIVERPOOL 3"   40 CHAPEL STREET, LIVERPOOL 3   Telephone: CENtral 1653-1654

DAILY SAILINGS

Liverpool to Llandudno and Menai Bridge

From Sat. 24th May to Thurs. 11th Sept. 1958

(SUBJECT TO ALTERATION WITHOUT NOTICE)

SUNDAYS INCLUDED

From PRINCES LANDING STAGE LIVERPOOL (weather and other circumstances permitting)

"ST. TUDNO" OR "ST. SEIRIOL"

Leaving		Each Day	
LIVERPOOL	...	10.45	a.m.
LLANDUDNO	due	1.05	p.m.
,,	dep.	1.15	p.m.
MENAI BRIDGE	due	2.40	p.m.

Leaving		Each Day	
MENAI BRIDGE	...	3.45	p.m.
LLANDUDNO	due	5.0	p.m.
,,	dep.	5.15	p.m.
LIVERPOOL	...	due 7.40	p.m.

N.B.—Passengers for Bangor, Caernarvon, Beaumaris, and other Anglesey Resorts—Crosville Bus Service from Menai Bridge.

DAILY THROUGH BOOKINGS FROM ALL PRINCIPAL RAILWAY STATIONS.

FARES—One Class Only (including Pier Tolls) between

	DAY EXCURSION RETURN	PERIOD RETURN	SINGLE
Liverpool and Llandudno	14/-	16/-	10/-
Liverpool and Menai Bridge	16/6	18/6	12/-

CHILDREN OVER 3 AND UNDER 14 YEARS HALF FARE.

CATERING—LUNCHEONS FROM 8/-; TEAS FROM 7/-.   CAFETERIA, BUFFETS AND REFRESHMENT BARS.

PRIVATE CABINS may be booked in advance.

DAY TRIP PARTIES SPECIALLY CATERED FOR AT REDUCED FARES IF PREVIOUSLY ARRANGED.

INTERCHANGE BOAT AND RAIL ARRANGEMENTS (BANK HOLIDAY EXCEPTED)

Passengers holding Day or Period Steamer Tickets have the option of returning by Rail on surrendering the Return Half Boat Tickets and on payment of the undermentioned rates, receiving single ticket to destination.

From LLANDUDNO (Day 8/6, Period 6/6)   From MENAI BRIDGE OR BANGOR (Day 10/4, Period 8/4)

Rail Passengers can return by steamer on payment of following supplementary charges at the Steamship Booking Offices, Pier Gates : Llandudno 7/-, Menai Bridge 8/-

Tickets may be obtained alongside vessels or in advance at Travel Agencies or Company's Office.

Bicycles 3/6 single journey, including Pier Tolls.   Luggage in Advance for Llandudno or Menai Bridge, or vice versa, 5,6 per package, collected and delivered (Local Liverpool area, 6/3 per package). Personal Luggage free of charge.

All Tickets are issued, Passengers and Goods carried, subject to the Company's Conditions of Carriage as exhibited at the Company's Offices and on the Vessels.

For all further particulars apply Travel Agencies; or **The Liverpool & North Wales S.S. Co. Ltd.**, 40 Chapel Street, Liverpool, 3

Souvenir Guide 1/-

FOR AFTERNOON SAILINGS SEE OTHER SIDE

1958 summer sailing list for the Liverpool & North Wales Steamship sailings from Liverpool to Llandudno and Menai Bridge.

COASTAL CRUISING ASSOCIATION

SPECIAL SPRING CRUISE

Liverpool and North Wales

(LLANDUDNO AND MENAI BRIDGE)

SATURDAY 15th MAY 1971

by M.V. BALMORAL

Depart from					Return time
LIVERPOOL (Princes Stage)	...	...	...	10 00	20 30
LLANDUDNO	...	...	...	13 15	17 30
MENAI BRIDGE	...	...	...	14 30	16 00

Thence cruise passing under Menai Suspension Bridge and Britannia Railway Bridge and viewing Port Dinorwic. Cruise departs Menai Bridge 14 45 and returns 15 45.

DAY RETURN FARES:

			Booked in Advance	Booked on day
From LIVERPOOL to LLANDUDNO	...	...	£1.50	£1.75
From LIVERPOOL to MENAI BRIDGE	...	...	£2.00	£2.25
From LIVERPOOL to MENAI STRAITS CRUISE	...	£2.25	£2.50
From LLANDUDNO to MENAI BRIDGE	...	...	80p	80p
From LLANDUDNO to MENAI STRAITS CRUISE	...	£1.10	£1.10
CRUISE from MENAI BRIDGE	...	...	50p	50p

Children 3-14 years half fare

Please note *Special Advance Fares* for tickets purchased prior to day of sailing. Advance Booking strongly advised *(Fares refunded if sailing cancelled)*

BOOKING ARRANGEMENTS

Tickets for the cruise and meals during voyage may be purchased by post only from:—
M. R. McRONALD, 48 WELLINGTON ROAD, BIRKENHEAD, L43 2JF

Steamer tickets may also be purchased alongside the ship on 15th May (subject to availability) or in advance from:—

FOR FURTHER INFORMATION SEE OVER

Coastal Cruising Association special spring cruise from Liverpool to North Wales on 15 May 1971.

B&I Line brochures.

1968-1969 B+I LINE

EXCURSIONS

LIVERPOOL
to DUBLIN

BY THE NEW CAR FERRY
m/v "MUNSTER"

19th NOVEMBER 1968 to 17th MAY 1969

(Except during the period
19th December 1968 to 1st January 1969. Also 3rd April 1969)

ONE CLASS **59/-** RETURN

DAY

DEPART LIVERPOOL (CARRIERS DOCK)
every TUESDAY and THURSDAY

Return from DUBLIN (FERRYPORT) the following day

WEEK-END

DEPART LIVERPOOL (CARRIERS DOCK)
every SATURDAY

Return from DUBLIN (FERRYPORT) the following Monday

Embarkation at both ports from 20·00 hours

Vessel sails at 22·15 hours

Apply — B+I LINE
COAST LINES LIMITED (Agents)

Reliance House, Water Street, Liverpool
L2 8TS

Telephone : 051-236 5464

Passengers, Vehicles and Luggage are only carried subject to the Company's
standard conditions of carriage as exhibited in the Company's Offices and on
board their vessels.

Robert McGee & Co. Ltd, 19 Old Hall Street, Liverpool, 3.

BELFAST STEAMSHIP CO. LTD.

NEW DRIVE—ON/DRIVE—OFF CAR FERRY

LIVERPOOL — BELFAST — LIVERPOOL

SUNDAY SAILINGS

in each direction

From 9th JULY to 17th SEPTEMBER 1967

FOR PASSENGERS WITH OR WITHOUT CARS.

Sailing Tickets necessary 23rd & 30th July, 6th August Liverpool-Belfast

NOT required Belfast-Liverpool

SAILINGS
FROM LIVERPOOL
Vehicles required at
    Car Ferry Terminal.
South West Princes Dock   Not later than 20.00
Passengers embark   20.00 to 21.30
Sailing time   21.45
Belfast arrival   07.00

SAILINGS
FROM BELFAST
Vehicles required at
    Car Ferry Terminal.
Donegall Quay   Not later than 18.30
Passengers embark 19.00 to 20.15
Sailing time   20.30
Liverpool arrival 07.00

Applications to :—

COAST LINES LTD. (Agents)
Reliance House,   227 Regent Street,
Water Street,   London, W. 1.
Liverpool, 2.   Telephone: REGent 6627
Telephone: CENtral 4921 Grams: " Comfyships,
Grams: " Afloat "   London, W. 1."
Telex: 62393

BELFAST STEAMSHIP CO. LTD.
94 High Street,
Belfast.
Telephone : 23636
Grams: " Passenger,"
    Telex: 74451.

Or the Motoring Organisations and Principal Travel Agents.

nightly PASSENGER services
Sundays excepted

LIVERPOOL to & from BELFAST

BELFAST S.S.CO.LTD

Belfast Steamship Company sailing lists.

Regular Direct Container Services Operating From The Container Terminal
1971

Line	Atlantic Container Line
Service	USA – Atlantic, weekly
Owner/Agent	Cunard-Brocklebank Ltd

Line	Ellerman Lines
Service	Portugal, weekly
Owner/Agent	Ellerman & Papayanni Lines Ltd

Line	Head Line/Canadian Pacific (Joint Service)
Service	Canada, every three weeks
Owner/Agent	G. Heyn & Sons (GB) Ltd

Line	MacAndrews Line
Service	Spain, weekly
Owner/Agent	MacAndrews & Co. Ltd

Line	Sealand Service Inc.
Service	USA – Atlantic, weekly
Owner/Agent	Ferrymasters Ltd

Line	United States Line
Service	USA – Atlantic, weekly
Owner/Agent	United States Lines

Darinian Ellerman & Papayanni Line 1947 1,533grt, 83m x 13m, 12kt Renamed Kostandis Fotinos in 1970, Tania Maria in 1972 and Nektarios in 1974. On 16 April 1978 she ran aground off Perim Island on a voyage from Aden and was abandoned.

Inishowan Head G. Heyn & Sons 1965
9,101grt, 148m x 20m, 15kt
Converted to a container ship in 1970 and renamed Cast Beaver in 1973. In 1977 she reverted back to Inishowan Head and became Sunhermine in 1979 and Catalina in 1982. She was broken up at Busan in 1986.

Velarde Mac Andrews Line 1957
2,055grt, 102m x 14m, $15\frac{1}{2}$kt
Renamed Sailor Prince in 1970, Zenit in 1971 and Nadir in 1973. Arrived at Split to be broken up on 27 April 1987.

Sungate (1954/5,795grt) of Saguenay Shipping discharges grain at the Homepride Flour Mills in the East Float at Birkenhead.

Steamship Service Berth Appropriation

Berth		
Alexandra Branch No.1, North		Furness Withy & Co. Ltd
Alexandra Branch No.1, South		Ellerman & Papayanni Lines Ltd
Alexandra Branch No.2, North	W. end	West Coast Stevedoring Co. Ltd
Alexandra Branch No.2, South	E. end	Blue Star Line Ltd
	E end	Liverpool Grain Storage & Transit Co. Ltd
Alexandra Branch No.3, North	Mid & W. end	Open Quay
		Clan Line Steamers Ltd (Discharging Berths)
Alexandra Branch No.3, South		Lamport & Holt Line Ltd
		Empresa Lineas Maritimas Argentinas (Lamport & Holt Line Ltd – Agents)
Alexandra Dock West side	S.end	Lamport & Holt Line Ltd
	Mid	Hall Line (Discharging Berth)
	N. end	Cunard Brocklebank Line
Bramley-Moore Dock	E. end	M.D. & H.B. Cargo Handling

Dock	Side	Operator / Service
South side	Mid & W. end	MacAndrews & Co. Ltd
Bramley-Moore Dock	E. side	Rough Cargo Berth
Bramley-Moore Dock	W. side	MacAndrews & Co. Ltd
Brocklebank Dock	W. side	M.D. & H.B. Cargo Handling
Brocklebank Branch North side	E. end	Elder Dempster Lines Ltd
	W.end	(West African Services)
Brocklebank Branch, South side	E. end	Ocean Port Services
	W. end	Guinea Gulf Line Ltd
Brunswick Dock, East side	N.end	Liverpool Grain Storage &Transit Co. Ltd
Brunswick Dock West side (NR)	Mid	Palm Line Ltd
	S.end	(West African Services)
	N.end	Limerick Steamship Co. Ltd.
	S.end	Elder Dempster Lines Ltd
Canada Dock. West side	Mid & N. end	M.D. & H.B. Cargo Handling
	S. end	A.E. Smith Coggins Ltd
Canada Branch No.1, North		Pacific Steam Navigation Co.
Canada Branch No.1, South		Port of Liverpool Stevedoring Co. Ltd
Canada Branch No.2. North		Thos & Jas. Harrison Ltd
Canada Branch No.2, South		Thos. & Jas. Harrison Ltd
Canada Branch No.3, North		A.E. Smith Coggins Ltd
Canada Branch No.3 South		F.C.Strick & Co.(Liverpool) Ltd
Canning Dock. East side	S. end	Open Quay (Rough Cargo)
Canning Dock. West side	N. end	Unallocated (Golfo Line using-Houlder Bros. & Co. Ltd – Agents)
Carriers Dock	North side	(B & I Car Ferry Terminal) M.D. & H.B Cargo Handling
Carriers Dock	South side	Rough Cargo Berth
Coburg Dock. North side		Isle of Man S.P. Co. Ltd
Coburg Dock. South side		Ireman Stevedoring Services Ltd (Containers)
Gladstone Branch No.1 N. side		Canadian Pacific S.S. Co. Ltd
Gladstone Branch No.1 S. side		Blue Funnel Line Ltd (Imports)
Gladstone Branch No.2 North side		Federal Steam Navigation Co. Ltd
Gladstone Branch No.2 S side	E. end	Blue Funnel Line Ltd (Exports)
Gladstone Container Terminal	W. end	Ocean Port Services Ltd
Gladstone Dock North side	N. end	M.D. & H.B. Cargo Handling
Gladstone Dock West side	Mid & S. end	Under Reconstruction
		Out of Commission
		Open Quay
Harrington Dock East side	N. end	Ocean Port Services Ltd
	S. end	Trafrume Line
		(Leinster & Co. (L'pool) Ltd Agents)
Harrington Dock West side	N.end	Booker Line Ltd

Berth	Position	Occupier
Herculaneum Branch Dock	Middle	Booth S.S. Co. Ltd
Herculaneum Branch Dock	S end	West Coast Stevedoring Co. Ltd
Herculaneum Branch Dock	E. side	Oil Quay
Herculaneum Branch Dock	W. side	Oil Quay
Hornby Container Terminal	W. end	M.D. & H.B. Cargo Handling
Hornby Dock North side		Geest Industries Ltd
Hornby Dock South side		Port of Liverpool Stevedoring (Co. Ltd)
Hornby Dock West side		Ellerman & Papayanni Lines Ltd
Hornby Dock East side		M.D. & H.B. Cargo Handling
Huskisson Branch No.3 North	E. end	Bulk Sugar (Huskisson Transit Co. Ltd)
Huskisson Branch No.3 North	Mid & W. end	A.E. Smith Coggins Ltd
Huskisson Branch No.3		New Zealand Shipping Co. Ltd and Shaw Savill & Albion Ltd
Huskisson Branch No.1 North	E. end	Cunard Steamship Co. Ltd
Huskisson Branch No.1 North	W. end	Open Quay
Huskisson Branch No.1 South		Cunard Steamship Co. Ltd
Huskisson Dock. West side		A.E. Smith Coggins Ltd
Kings Dock No.1 North side	Mid & W. end	A.E. Smith Coggins Ltd
Kings Dock No.1 North side	E. end	Open Quay. (Rough Cargo)
Kings Dock No.1 South side		A.E. Smith Coggins Ltd
Kings Dock No.2. North side		M.D. & H.B. Cargo Handling
Kings Dock No.2	E. end	Ellerman & Papayanni Lines Ltd
Kings Dock No.2	Mid	A.E. Smith Coggins Ltd
Kings Dock No.2	W. end	M.D. & H.B. Cargo Handling
Langton Branch North side		Bugsier Line
Langton Dock North side		Unallocated
Langton Dock West side		Coast Lines Ltd
Nelson Dock West side (NR)		Coast Lines Ltd
Nelson Dock East side (NR)		British & Irish S.P. Co. Ltd
Nelson Dock North side (NR)	E. end	Belfast S.S. Co. Ltd (Car Ferry Terminal)
Princes Dock East side		A.E. Smith Coggins Ltd
Princes Dock West side		West Coast Stevedoring Co. Ltd
Queens Branch No.1 South side	W. end	Open Quay (Rough Cargo)
Queens Branch No.1 North side	Mid	A.E. Smith Coggins Ltd
Queens Branch No.1 North side	E. end	A.E. Smith Coggins Ltd
Queens Branch No.2 North	N. end	West Coast Stevedoring Co. Ltd
Queens Branch No.2 South	S. end	A.E. Smith Coggins Ltd
Queens Dock East side		Unallocated
Salthouse Dock. East side		M.D. & H.B. Cargo

Location		Operator
Sandon Dock South side		M.D. & H.B. Cargo Handling
Sandon Dock East side		Cunard Steamship Co. Ltd
Sandon Dock North side		Ulster S.S. Co. Ltd (Head Line)
		M.D. & H.B. Cargo Handling
Toxteth Dock East side		Moss Hutchison Line Ltd
Toxteth Dock West side		Elder Dempster Lines Ltd (West African Services)
Trafalgar Dock West side	N. end	A. Guinness, Son & Co. (Park Royal) Ltd
	S. end	Irish & Mersey. S.S. Co. Ltd
Trafalgar Dock East side		Coast Lines Ltd
Trafalgar Branch Dock North side (NR)		Coast Lines Ltd
Trafalgar Branch Dock East side (NR)		Coast Lines Ltd
Trafalgar Branch Dock South side		Open Quay
Victoria Dock North side NR		Coast Lines Ltd
Victoria Dock East side		Coast Lines Ltd
	E. end NR	Waterloo Transport Co. Ltd
Victoria Dock South side	W. end NR	Open Quay
Wapping Basin East side		M.D. & H.B. Cargo Handling
Wellington Dock North side		M.D. & H.B. Cargo Handling
Wellington Dock South side		M.D. & H.B. Cargo Handling
East Waterloo Dock		Waterloo Transport Co. Ltd

Birkenhead Docks

Location	Operator
Bidston Dock North side	Iron Ore Berth (Rea Ltd)
Bidston Dock South side	Unallocated
East Float	
East Quay	T.&J. Brocklebank Ltd
North side, Mortar Mill Quay	(Nippon Yusen Kaisha Gellatly Hankey & Co. Ltd – Agents)
E&W Towers (Grain Storage)	Liverpool Grain Storage & Transit Co. Ltd
(grain Berth)	Ranks Buchanan Mill
North side No.1 Duke Street	Unallocated
North side No.3 Duke Street	Unallocated
Cathcart Street	Blue Funnel Line Ltd
Vittoria Wharf Terminal	Clan Line Steamers Ltd
Vittoria Dock South side	Blue Funnel Line Ltd
Alfred Dock South side	Unallocated
Alfred Dock North side	Open Quay

West Float (North side)

Nos. 1 & 2 Sections		Bibby/Henderson Lines
Nos. 3 & 4 Sections		Hall/City Lines
No.5 Section		Harrison/Hall Lines
Petroleum Quay		Open
Grain Berth		Spillers Uveco Mill

Lewis' Quay Clan Line Steamers Ltd

W. end Oil Quay
E. end Oil Quay

West Float (South side)

Ilchester Wharf		Oil Quay
Grain Berth		Spillers Beaufort Road Mill
Grain Berth		Ranks Ocean Mill
Cavendish Quay	W. end	87 Ton Crane
East end (Rea's Cavendish Wharf)		Rough Cargo Berths (Rea Ltd)

Daghestan Common Brothers 1960
11,204grt, 160m x 21m, 15½kt
She was sold in 1976 and renamed Lovinda and Mercury in 1981. On 10 June 1982, on a voyage from Varna to Manila, she suffered an engine room fire south off Rhodes. She was towed to Piraeus where she was laid up. In 1987 she was broken up at Aliga.

Shipping Operators 2006

A rare sighting in 2000 at the Royal Seaforth Container Terminal of two Atlantic Container Line vessels as they load cargo for North American ports.

Atlantic Container Line
Type: container/ro-ro
Ports: Halifax N.S.; New York; Baltimore; Portsmouth; with feeder services to Bermuda via New York.
Berth: R.S.C.T.
Frequency: weekly

Baco Liner
Type: timber and forest products
Ports: West Africa
Berth: R.S.C.T.
Frequency: monthly

Borchard Line
Type: container
Ports: Ashdod; Haifa
Berth: R.S.C.T.
Frequency: weekly

Britannic Timber Ltd
Type: timber and forest products
Ports: Estonia
Frequency: monthly

Canada Maritime
Type: container/ro-ro
Ports: Montreal; all Mid-West US destinations
Berth: R.S.C.T.
Frequency: weekly

Cast Container Line
Type: container/ro-ro
Ports: Montreal; all Mid-West US destinations
Berth: R.S.C.T.
Frequency: weekly

C.C.N.I.-Condor Express Line
Type: break bulk
Ports: Chile; Peru; Bolivia; Ecuador; Colombia
Berth: Royal Seaforth Dock

CMA-CGM
Type: container/ro-ro
Ports: all destinations
Berth: R.S.C.T.
Frequency: weekly

Coastal Container Line
Type: container
Ports: Dublin
Berth: R.S.C.T.
Frequency: daily Mon-Sat
Ports: Belfast
Frequency: Tues, Thurs, Sat

Compania Libra de Navegacao
Ports: East Coast South America

Compania Sud-Americana de Vapores
Type: break bulk/containers
Ports: Chile; Ecuador; Peru; Bolivia

Ellerman/KNSM & Zim Joint Service
Type: container
Ports: Dublin; Malta; Piraeus; Limassol; Ashdod; Haifa; Salerno
Berth: R.S.C.T.
Frequency: every ten days

Ellerman Portuguese Service
Type: container
Ports: Lisbon, Leixoes, Gibraltar
Berth: R.S.C.T.
Frequency: weekly

Eucon
Type: container
Ports: Dublin
Berth: R.S.C.T.
Frequency: six days a week

Eukor 21 Car Carriers
Type: ro-ro
Ports: Japan; Middle East
Frequency: monthly

Finsa
Type: timber and forest products
Ports: Spain
Frequency: every ten days

Freightliners
Type: container
Ports: Dublin; Belfast
Berth: R.S.C.T.
Frequency: six days a week

Mor Canada *Baltic Shipping 1979*
17,304grt, 170m x 25m, 19kt
Built as Nikolay Golovanov and renamed Mor Canada in 1994.

Cast Privilege *Cast Container Line 1978*
26,383grt, 219m x 31m, 23kt
Built as Dart Canada, renamed Canadian Explorer in 1981, OOCL Bravery in 1990, Canmar Bravery in 1998 and Cast Privilege in 1999.

Gearbulk (UK) Ltd
- Type: timber and forest products
- Ports: East Canada; US
- Frequency: monthly

Gorthon Lines AB
- Type: timber and forest products
- Ports: East Coast Canada; US
- Frequency: monthly

Gracechurch Container Line
- Type: container
- Ports: Lisbon; Leixoes; Malta; Piraeus; Alexandria; Limassol; Salerno; Istanbul; Izmir.
- Berth: R.S.C.T.
- Frequency: weekly
- Ports: Tunis; Limassol; Ashdod; Haifa; Palermo; Salerno.

Hamburg Sud
- Type: container/ro-ro
- Ports: South America
- Berth: R.S.C.T.
- Frequency: monthly
- Type: break bulk
- Ports: Colombia; Chile; Ecuador; Peru; Bolivia.
- Frequency: every nine to ten days

Hapag-Lloyd (UK) Ltd
- Type: container/ro-ro
- Ports: Halifax N.S; New York; Baltimore; Portsmouth; Portland (Maine); Boston; Philadelphia via Halifax; Bermuda via New York.
- Berth: R.S.C.T.
- Frequency: weekly

Hyundai Merchant Marine
- Type: break bulk
- Ports: Far East

Independent Container Line
- Type: container/ro-ro
- Ports: Chester; Richmond; all Eastern Seaboard destinations.
- Berth: R.S.C.T.
- Frequency: weekly

Islamic Republic of Iran Shipping Line
- Type: break bulk
- Ports: Iranian and Persian Gulf ports
- Berth: R.S.C.T.
- Frequency: monthly

Isle Of Man Steam Packet Co. Ltd
- Type: ro-ro
- Ports: Douglas, Isle of Man
- Frequency: twice daily in summer, once daily in winter

'K' Line – Condor Express Service
- Type: break bulk
- Ports: Chile; Peru; Bolivia; Ecuador; Colombia

Kent Line
- Type: break bulk/container
- Ports: East Coast Canada; USA
- Frequency: monthly

MacAndrews & Co. Ltd
- Type: container
- Ports: Bilbao; Lisbon; Leixoes
- Berth: R.S.C.T.
- Frequency: Portugal: weekly / Spain: twice weekly

Magellan Service
- Type: break bulk
- Ports: East/West Coast South America
- Berth: R.S.C.T.

Maple Line
- Type: lumber, forest products and metals
- Ports: Gros Cacouna and other St Lawrence ports
- Berth: Royal Seaforth Forest Products Terminal
- Frequency: every eight weeks

Marfret (UAL)
- Type: container
- Ports: Montreal and all Mid-West USA
- Berth: R.S.C.T.
- Frequency: weekly

Mediterranean Shipping Company
- Type: container/ro-ro
- Ports: all global destinations
- Berth: R.S.C.T.
- Frequency: weekly

Cast Wolf Cast Container Line 1989
23,761grt, 202m x 28m, 17kt
Built as Norasia Singa she became Cast Wolf in 1994. Sold in 2005 and renamed Thorstream.

CCNI Potrerillos CCNI Line 1997
28,148grt, 185m x 32m, $15\frac{1}{2}$kt
Built as Lara Rickmers and renamed CCNI Potrerillos in 1997.

118

Melbridge Container Line
Type   container
Ports   Caribbean; Central America
Berth   R.S.C.T.
Frequency every two weeks

New Falcomar Line
Ports   Liverno
Berth   S 3 Huskisson
Frequency every two weeks

Normandy UK Line
Type   timber and forest products
Ports   Rouen
Frequency every two weeks

Norse Merchant Ferries
Type   ro-ro
Ports   Belfast; Dublin
Berth   Twelve Quays
Frequency twenty-six sailings a week

Northern Shipping Company
Type   break bulk
          timber and forest products
Ports   Arkhangelsk
Berth   R.S.C.T.
Frequency monthly

Oceanic Cargo Lines
Type   break bulk
Ports   Apapa; Lagos; Tema; Abidjan

OOCL
Type   container/ro-ro
Ports   Montreal and all Mid-West US
          destinations
Berth   R.S.C.T.
Frequency weekly

P&O European Ferries
Type   ro-ro
Ports   Dublin
Berth   Gladstone
Frequency twice a day

Panocean Line
Type   timber and forest products
Ports   Far East
Frequency Monthly

Price & Pierce
Type   timber and forest products
Ports   Latvia
Frequency every six weeks

Sea Logistics Line
Ports   Estonia; Latvia
Frequency monthly

Sontrade Line
Type   timber and forest products
Ports   Portugal and Latvia
Berth   R.S.C.T.
Frequency fortnightly

Trac World
Type   timber and forest products
Ports   St Lawrence
Frequency bi-monthly

Transways Shipping (U.K.) Ltd
Type   timber and forest products
Ports   Arkhangelsk
Frequency monthly

Tropimar Line
Type   timber and forest products
Ports   North Brazil

Ultra Iscont Lines
Type   container
Ports   Israel; Limassol
Berth   R.S.C.T.
Frequency Weekly

Wallenius Wilhelmsen Lines (UK)
Type   ro-ro
Ports   Halifax; Newark; Baltimore;
          Portsmouth
Frequency weekly

Zim
Type   container
Ports   Tunis; Piraeus; Limassol;
          Ashdod; Haifa; Salerno
Frequency weekly

(R.S.C.T. – Royal Seaforth Container Terminal)

Christopher Meeder (1976/2,154grt) and Adele J (1979/3,917grt) loading at the short-sea berths at the Liverpool Container Terminal.

Finch Arrow, Gearbulk Limited 1984
26,130grt, 183m x 29m, 13kt
Built as Francois L.D. and renamed Finch Arrow in 1990.

Worldler Shipping's Great Lake (1991/25,905 grt) unloading steel sections at Gladstone Dock in 1999. Later that year she was sold and renamed Asante.

Splendour Of The Seas (1996/69,490grt) moves slowly down the river and heads for her next port of call in Scotland.

Maria Gorthon, Gorthon Lines 1984
13,533grt, 156m x 22m, 15kt

Gracechurch Planet, Gracechurch Container Line 1994
4,984grt, 116m x 19m, $16\frac{1}{2}$kt.

Raven Arrow 25,063grt. Gearbulk 1981
178m x 29m 15 kt.

P&O Ferries Jetliner (1996/4,565grt.) heads through the Birkenhead dock system on her way to a winter overhaul in Bidston Drydock. She operated on P&O's Larne to Cairnryan service until 17 June 2000 and was sailing from Semarang in Indonesia the following year.

Independent Action, Independent Container Line 1992
14,867grt, 167m x 25m, 17kt

Seacat Isle Of Man, Isle of Man Steam Packet 1991
3,003grt, 74m x 26m, 35kt
She was built as Hoverspeed France, became Sardegna Express and Hoverspeed France again in 1992, Seacat Boulogne and Seacat Isle Of Man in 1994, Seacat Norge in 1996 and Seacat Isle Of Man again in 1997. In 2005 she operated as Sea Express 1 for Irish Sea Express but this service closed after several months because of rising fuel costs.

Swedish Orient Lines Tyrusland (1978/20,882grt) loads cargo at the Royal Seaforth Container Terminal.

Atlantic Cartier (1985/58,358grt) swings in the river and prepares to dock at Gladstone Dock.

Forest Atlantic, *Rederi AB Swan 1973*
10,522grt, 146m x 20m, 16kt

Melbridge Christine, *Melbridge Container Line 1984*
9,764grt, 149m x 22m, 17kt

Merchant Venture, Norse Merchant Ferries 1979
6,056grt, 119m x 20m, 17kt
Built as Farman and became Med Adriatica in 1982, Argentea in 1985, Merchant Isle and Merchant Venture in 1987. In 2003 she was renamed Warsun.

Lagan Viking, Norse Merchant Ferries 1997
21,500grt, 186m x 26m, 24kt

European Envoy, P&O European Ferries 1979
18,653grt 150m x 22m 19k
Built as Ibex, renamed Norsea in 1980, Norsky in 1986, Ibex in 1995 and European Envoy in 1998. She was sold to Kystlink in 2004 and renamed Envoy.

Superseacat Three, Seacontainers 1999
4,700grt, 100m x 17m, 38kt

Arabian Express, Vroom BV 1977
10,459grt, 147m x 22m, 14k
Built as Adelphi Yemelos and renamed Arabian Express in 1984.

Zim Britain Zim Line 1978
14,050grt, 157m x 25m, 19k.
She was renamed Britain Star in 2005.